LETTERS TO DR. WIGGY

DR. ELLEN KRUMHOLZ MANDEL

ISBN: 1539103994
ISBN 13: 9781539103998

Dedicated to Dr. Susan L Maxam("Dr. Wiggy")
In Memory of my parents, Marvin and Shirley Krumholz

Contents

Acknowledgments

There are many people who assisted in bringing this book to fruition. First the editorial team at CreateSpace, with Tim Male at the helm, had the challenging job of helping this phobic and illiterate computer author press the right buttons to send her work forth.

Rockland Instant Copy Center (Keith, Alex, and Paula) turned my e-mails into an MS Word document. Many thanks!

Thanks to my dear friend and former student Caesar (Winston) Vera, Document Services at Pace University, who made copies of my work and cheered me on.

Kudos to my wonderful friends who became instant reviewers. These willing and unwilling reviewers gave their honest opinions, suggestions, and advice. They included Dr. Diane Cypkin, Dr. Alan J. Chernick, Mel Maslansky, Fred Grayson, and my first cousin-friend Bud Rosenthal.

Everyone should be blessed to have a sister like Susan (Sooz); I can't thank her or celebrate her enough for helping me and supporting me with almost every aspect involved in this book's preparation. She spent hours and hours with the computer, helping me organize my chapters, and generating ideas. She even added two vignettes about her hysterical issues with her hair.

Thanks to my brother-in-law, Dr. Martin D. Shulman, who is more like a brother and still insists through the writing of the whole book that he yells at me with love.

My nuclear family is at the top of my list for thank-yous, love, and support.

Special thanks to my wonderful husband of forty-eight years, Dr. David N. Mandel; my son, Leigh E. Mandel; my daughter, Susannah Mandel Brill; her husband, Sam Brill; and my two amazing grandsons, the Brill Boys—Matthew Steven and his brother and sidekick, Jacob Benjamin. This group is truly my raison d'etre, and I couldn't love them more than I do.

A final thank-you goes to Dr. Susan L. Maxam (Dr. Wiggy), the "queen of survivors," who managed to get through her breast cancer with dignity and grace. She continues to serve as a role model to all of us who face adversity. Brava!

Dr. Wiggy's Foreward

Both of my parents and all four of my grandparents succumbed to cancer over the past decade. Then in 2011, I was diagnosed with breast cancer. However, the last thing I sought from others was sympathy. I simply wanted to recover and move on so that I could continue with my life's mission of making a difference in the lives of others. So, among the first people I called was Dr. Mandel (aka Dr. Piggy). I knew I (aka Dr. Wiggy) could count on her for whatever support I needed, however unconventional.

Soon after surgery, my Oncologist ordered months of chemotherapy, which helped <u>rid</u> my body of cancer. As a complementary "treatment," Dr. Mandel "ordered" a hefty dose of laughter through hilarious snippets of her life, which <u>infused</u> my body with endorphins (otherwise known as "happy hormones!). These snippets were delivered to my Inbox on a near daily basis throughout my entire recovery. Who, in the throes of chemo would practically (and gleefully) run to her computer in the morning? I did, because even though I was physically miserable and felt like I was imploding, I knew Dr. Mandel's emails were so funny that they would make me forget my physical woes and release those all-important endorphins into my body! In fact, I would sit at my computer and laugh hysterically from reading side-splitting stories of Dr. Mandel's life!

Research has shown that laughter is the perfect elixir. Humor truly does heal the soul. I am living proof of this and I have Dr. Mandel to thank for that!

Dr. Mandel spent nearly 40 years teaching public speaking classes in the wee hours of the morning when most of the world (especially students) were fast asleep. Yet, her classes closed practically before they were opened for registration not only because she was a fabulous professor but because she infused humor throughout every session. In fact, her laughter therapy is legendary at Pace University, as is her commitment to supporting any and all cancer research, fundraising and awareness initiatives.

After I recovered from cancer, Dr. Mandel was diagnosed with Leukemia. Although she will have to live the rest of her life with this illness, she does not let it stop her from living life to the fullest, making others laugh, and giving of herself to every person she encounters every single day. She also still dedicates an enormous amount of time and energy helping foundations such as Susan G. Komen and American Cancer Society as they continue searching for a cure for cancer and supporting those who have it.

I am eternally grateful to Dr. Mandel for being a key factor in my recovery and for publishing this book to continue spreading laughter to all who read it!! So, whether you are recuperating from a serious illness or a common cold, or you simply want to fall off your chair guffawing over and over again, read this book!

The Inception of Dr. Wiggy

From: Mandel, Dr. Ellen
Sent: Friday, December 1, 2011, 10:13 a.m.
To: Maxam, Dr. Susan L.
Subject: No more teddy bears

My dear Sue,

Hope that you are feeling well and, of course, fighting the fight. I want to fight right alongside you! I think that you have received enough teddy bears in ridiculous costumes from me to last a lifetime. I have therefore decided, quite on the spur of the moment, to send you funny little snippets or vignettes dealing with just about everything in an attempt to elicit a chuckle from you during these sucky times. This is not about cancer but rather about laughing.

Since I was a wee lass (I was never a wee lass), and being a cross between Calamity Jane and Gracie Allen, I have told stories about my friends, family, mishaps, the world we live in, parenting, and grandparenting to anyone who would listen. These stories always brought about laughter and sometimes tears from the listening audience. I will be happy to share them with you. Since it is common knowledge that my computer skills place me in the imbecile category, I will e-mail each snippet to you as often as I can.

The names of the characters (and that they are) will not be changed to protect the guilty. Au contraire. Let them all suck it up.

Major Characters

1) Dr. David Mandel—husband and gifted psychologist. Hasn't been wrong in over forty years (adored).
2) Leigh Even Mandel—oldest child, forty-one years old, who will be fully matured and married after I'm dead (adored).
3) Susannah Mandel Brill—beloved daughter too light for heavy work and too heavy for light work. Almost my clone, only a little less of a hysteric (thank God).
4) Sam Brill—Susannah's husband and my adored son-in-law. Sam asked Leigh right before Susannah and his wedding what he did to deserve his bride. Leigh replied, "I don't know what the hell you must have done."
5) Matthew Steven Brill and Jacob Benjamin Brill—adored grandsons who have special keys to my heart and my pocketbook.
6) Susan Krumholz Shulman—adored and brilliant sister who is pragmatic, has good judgment, and is, unfortunately, sane.
7) Dr. Martin D. Shulman—adored brother-in-law, who is always supportive, sometimes critical, and always amazed that his wife and his sister-in-law have been reminiscing for over fifty years.

Two more important things, my dear Sue.

1) Since you have lost your hair and have so many beautiful scarves and wigs, you will be addressed as "Dr. Wiggy."
2) As a rehabilitated bulimic with body dysmorphia I will sign my e-mails "Dr. Piggy."

May the e-mails begin!

Love you,
Dr. Piggy

CHAPTER 1

Family and Friends

From: Mandel, Dr. Ellen
Sent: Monday, December 4, 2011, 7:07 p.m.
To: Maxam, Dr. Susan L.
Subject: Am I my sister's keeper?

My dear Dr. Wiggy,

I saw my delicious grandsons late this afternoon, and they are getting so big.

Not their height, mind you, but their vocabularies and ability to conceptualize are excellent.

Another gift from God!

My daughter and son-in-law are doing a wonderful job!

Sometimes when I hear Susannah talking to the boys, it reminds me of my talking to her and her brother. Susannah wants Matthew to watch out for his brother, and I expected Leigh to watch out for Susannah, but in my house watching out for pushed the envelope. They killed each other!

My mother too, insisted that I take care of my sister.

In my day, Saturday afternoon was movie day.

For only thirty cents you could see a double feature and twenty-five color cartoons.

Most candy was six cents or twelve cents, and bonbons were a quarter.

Kids went by themselves, little siblings accompanying big siblings.

Parents did not worry.

Kids sat in the children's section and were watched by the matron who always looked like the Wicked Witch of the East.

She was old, cranky, and flashed a big flashlight in your face if you talked even for a minute.

I never talked! I was deathly afraid of the matron!

"Sooz," my younger sister, was particularly fond of horror movies.

My mother made me "watch her" even though I protested.

Otherwise she couldn't go.

I spent my entire time that the horror movie was on under the seat!

To keep myself happy, I stuffed myself with Baby Ruths (those were fifteen cents, as I recall).

The few times that I came out, there would be blood and gore, and I hurried back under my seat until the show was finally over. As a little chub, it was a challenge to get under the seat, believe me.

A smarter girl would have gotten up and left, but I wasn't a smarter girl, and I had to watch my sister.

The story was a similar one when it came to horseback riding.

My mother would let Sooz go only if I went along.

If I didn't go, she couldn't go, so I went.

Sooz was little and got a cute little horse.

I wasn't so big, but I got a mutation, giganto-horse.

Giganto-horse was a purplish-pink color.

He didn't look well, but then, neither did I.

Sooz's horse was making horse sounds, moving his head and neck.

He demonstrated horse behavior.

My horse demonstrated sick behavior—no expression on his face, didn't move his legs or shake his head.

The leader of this horseback-riding extravaganza asked if we were ready to ride on the trail.

I said no, and we moved on to the trail.

Sooz was loving the experience.

She liked the horse, the horse liked her, and they both were moving along at a good clip.

Then there was me.

My horse was dragging his ass, and we didn't say a word to each other, but at least he was moving.

After about five minutes on the trail, we came to an intersection that we had to cross in order to continue on the trail.

The leader waited for each of us to cross, and when my horsie got to the middle of the intersection, he had had enough.

He stopped and wouldn't cross the street.

I called him one horse's ass after another, but he was going nowhere fast.

Finally the leader whispered something in his ear, and he took off like Secretariat with me on his back.

We were both screaming (the horse and I).

Alas, the leader saved us. He stopped the horse, I got off, and I have never been on a horse since, not even on a merry-go-round.

Well, my dear friend, I was a good sister even though my mother was wrongheaded when it came to my having to watch her.

But somehow, it worked out fine.

I have the best sister in the world, and in a much more normal, unassuming way, we always have and always will watch out for each other.

All my love,
Dr. Piggy

From: Mandel, Dr. Ellen
Sent: Monday February 20, 2012
To: Maxam, Dr. Susan L.
Subject: A Memorial to My Mother

Dear Dr. Wiggy,

Today was the *yarzeit* (anniversary according to the Jewish calendar) of my mother's passing away. She has been gone fourteen years, so long and so close to yesterday at the same time.

I am not a religious Jew by anyone's standards, least of all my own. But there are some traditions that I know I will always follow, until it is time to join them. This is my fantasy.

After my rabbi retired from the reform synagogue, we retired our membership. I don't miss it. I find that I like to pray in a smaller group, sometimes a group of only one.

I wasn't sure this morning, however, that I would be able to talk to either my God or my mother. I was distracted, self-absorbed, and tired from a lingering bout of bronchitis.

However, I entered the sanctuary, took off my coat, and grabbed a book. At first, just as I thought, nothing. And then this wonderfully sweet rabbi asked me whom I was there to remember. I gave him my mother's name in Hebrew—Sura Gisha bat Leah and Duvid (Shirley Gladys, daughter of my beloved Nanny Lillian and Pop-Pop David).

Then a miracle! As I gave the rabbi her name, my eyes filled with tears that soon dropped onto my cheeks. I was there to remember, to talk to my God and to my mother.

I had this very thing the previous week for my father, but it was so easy to talk to my dad. But this was my mother, who in recent years before her death was not so easy to talk to. But it was OK; perhaps what I couldn't say to her in life, I could say to her in death.

Nothing ever profound or terrible ever transpired between us. But she was critical of me and me of her. I held her too responsible for some things and not responsible enough for others. But that was so not the point.

"Thank you, Mother," I said, "for teaching me so many of life's lessons, for teaching me the meaning of family, for giving of yourself and showing me, in whatever shape or form you could, the importance of having God in my life."

My talk was interrupted by the rabbi who was bestowing a small honor on me. I would be given an *Aleah*(a special prayer when the ark was open and the Torah was being read). "This is for you today, Mom," I said to myself. "Here are some long-overdue praises for you, who often had little for yourself, but gave as much as you possibly could to your daughters in every way that you were capable of."

I chanted well. My voice was rich and beautiful. The congregation was still.

This daily nothing somehow had become such a big something for me.

I returned from the pulpit to my seat, tears welling up and once again falling onto my cheeks.

There was some relief of tension and feelings of joy having spoken to my mother and to God.

We will have this chat again, I promised myself, and perhaps more often. Still, I am floundering, still trying to find myself and like myself after all of these years, but now, I have more hope in my heart!

From: Mandel, Dr. Ellen
Sent: August 10, 2012, 2:25 p.m.
To: Maxam, Dr. Susan L.
Subject: Overnight camps of yesteryear and today

Dear Dr. Wiggy,

Know Joey will be fine.
Know that lump is benign.
Hope you laugh from this story of mine.

Soon little Suzie and Sally will be coming home from sleepaway camp.

Moms and dads will have their feathers all ruffled because their party is quite over.

My mother and her older sister, Gert, attended camp eighty-five years ago.

Sooz and I roared when we heard their hilarious stories.

Both girls weighed upward of two hundred pounds and were not "good lookers," as my grandfather admitted, when they were grown women.

Both were thrilled that they had their own father attest to this.

Both girls were very athletic and excelled at all the sports that were offered.

Their only problem was that their "avoir du pois" got in the way of their passing the boating test.

Both girls took the test innumerable times but could not manage to complete the tasks.

They had to get into the boat, take off their outer layer of clothes, jump in, save the dummy, put the dummy in their boat, and get back into the boat.

All was just great, until the part that they had to get back into the boat.

Because of their weight, the boat always capsized as they tried to get back in.

Thank God they had fabulous senses of humor and began to laugh uncontrollably.

My mother was the real camper, and my sister was just like her.

Tanta (aunt) Gert had terrible bouts of homesickness. She would write terrible letters home.

My aunt Cele, my mother's aunt and my great-aunt, whom I just adored, wrote to Aunt Gert and told her that it was so hot, they were frying eggs on the sidewalk.

She only wanted to come home to see the fried eggs.

I was cut from the same mold as my aunt Gert.

I carried on, even at day camp.

I wanted my mother, and I didn't even like her so much at that time.

Go figure.

Mother's camp and the assorted camps that Sooz and I were at were what camp was supposed to be.

Rustic, a little rugged, hot, damp, and muddy when it rained.

Food was lousy, and punch, or "bug juice," as it was called, was sugar and water with artificial flavoring.

Nobody died from it, and nobody complained.

At the canteen you spent a few cents every night, and nothing there was healthy—wonderful, but not healthy.

If you were homesick, nobody came for you.

You had to make the best of it.

I never made the best of anything (ask Sooz), but I was the exception to the rule.

So much the exception that when I was eighteen and a counselor at a sleepaway camp and had a bunch of eleven-year-olds, I was the only one who missed her mom!

Today, camp is a totally different story.

They can be as costly as $12,000 per camper.

That was more money than David and I made in our first year of marriage!

Appointments are made to buy camp clothes from a variety of clothiers.

Sneakers to insure great athletic prowess cost well over one hundred dollars.

A far cry from our Keds for $5.95 at Thom McAnn.

Many kids with the one-hundred-dollar sneakers are still sucky athletes.

Bunks are air-conditioned and look like the Courtyard Marriot Suites.

Children cannot be sent care packages from home.

This is understandable in today's world of assorted "crazies," unfortunately.

The parents gather with packages on the morning of visiting day.

Parents stand behind a line (having partaken in a breakfast spread beforehand) with baskets of goodies. The ropes are removed at 10:00 a.m., and the parents run up the hill to see their offspring.

If you happen to kill a few of the slower parents rushing up the hill into the arms of your child, so be it.

It couldn't be helped.

Well, the six or seven or eight weeks pass quickly, and sooner or later these happy campers arrive home

Many parents help their children adjust to the remaining few weeks before school by taking them on a family vacation.

It too is understandable.

They need a vacation from their vacation.

Other kids are not so lucky.

They have to rough it at home with their iPads, TVs, iPhones, and i-everything else.

That's it for now, my sweet Dr. Wiggy.
Love u

Never met a braver, more optimistic person in my life than you!
Dr. Piggy

From: Mandel, Dr. Ellen
Sent: Wednesday, February 13, 2013, 7:42 p.m.
To: Maxam, Dr. Susan L.
Subject: How I miss my crazy friend Ellen

Good evening, my dearest Dr. Wiggy,

First, my dear friend, we are having trouble finding a commencement speaker. Any leads?

I sent threatening letters to every member of my department.

Requirements were breathing, either on their own or with assistance.

I gave them permission to use bribery or kidnapping if necessary.

For the February break, Susannah, Sam, and the kids are going to a ranch that has pony rides, skiing, and a whole bunch of other frills, all for the low cost of $1,800 (for three days).

I told her that she could probably buy a horse for less than what the three days are costing them.

So happy that I taught her the value of money.

The fact that Matthew, the soon-to-be seven-year-old, and his short four-year-old brother, Jacob, don't want to ride ponies, has no effect on the trip at all. Neither of the boys ski either, for that matter.

Matthew says that horses stink, while Jake made the keen observation that horsies poop, and nobody wipes their tushies.

Should be quite a trip.

Good news—I am not going.

Rather, David and I will be in New City, and we have chosen to be the designated worriers. This worrying thing reminds me of a very dear friend of mine, who died as a young woman from cancer and who suffered from acute anxiety disorder.

You can imagine how bad she was, if she made me look like the mental health poster person.

You can imagine how bad she was when she selected me as her mentor for anxiety control.

I used the behavior-modification method.

I made her an anxiety schedule.

From nine to ten, she could worry only about our doctoral program.

Ten until eleven, her smoking.

Eleven to twelve, her boyfriend.

At three I told her to worry about whatever the hell she wanted to and keep repeating the schedule.

I don't think that my suggestions reduced her anxiety in the least, but it did turn her into one of the most organized and routinized crazy persons in the world.

I still miss my Ellen, but I don't miss her second ex-husband, who shall remain nameless.

Her first husband became a millionaire about three hours after she divorced him.

She waited seventeen years after that to meet "Mr. Wrong."

When I met him, I knew instantly that he was not for her, in any way.

This ex had a small boat, and Ellen decided when things started to go south that David and I should go with her and her husband for a boat ride under the Tappan Zee Bridge.

I explained that I really didn't want to go.

She told me it would help her marriage.

"How would it help your marriage," I asked, "if I get seasick under the Tappan Zee Bridge, or under any bridge for that matter?"

The nameless person needs to be socializing.

Send him to bingo, I suggested. No such luck.

David and I sailed with great trepidation away from the dock.

I am sure that you know who felt nauseous from the instant this boat trip was under way. My Ellen would have none of it.

Have a bagel, she offered.

"No, thank you," I replied. "Maybe later."

I moved over to the railing when she complained that I wasn't giving the unnamed person a chance to bond with me.

If you want bonding, I said, he can hold my head while I vomit my kishkas out.

About six weeks after this boat ride from hell, Ellen decided what we all knew right away—this man of hers was a disaster.

I wanted to give her as much support as possible because to me that is what being a friend involves.

I instructed her to call me anytime, night or day.

I expected that she would be calling often, and she did.

What I didn't expect was that the doorbell would ring one night after midnight.

Ellen greeted me by saying, "You will be so proud of me."

"Am I proud because you woke David and me out of a deep sleep? Because, frankly, proud isn't the way I am feeling now."

"How long will you be staying," I asked as she came in and made herself at home—my home, that is.

"Not more than four weeks," was her response.

And not a day shorter than four weeks it was.

Crazy friend, but a sweetie pie whom I still miss.

Love u,
Dr. Piggy

From: Mandel, Dr. Ellen
Sent: Sunday, August 11, 2013, 10:59 a.m.
To: Maxam, Dr. Susan L.
Subject: A new car for David

Good morning, Dr. Wiggy.

Hope everything is going well.

When will u be checking in with your oncologist?

The Marvin Krumholzes always bought two kinds of cars, as I recall: more used and less used.

There was no euphemism, such as "previously owned," which of course means "used."

This was all that we could afford.

As I have mentioned in other little vignettes, the first car I remember when I was three was Pop-Pop's 1949 green Buick Roadmaster, better known as the vomit mobile.

This was appropriately named because almost everybody in the family, but mainly me, vomited in it.

It was also fondly known as the circus car, holding eight for each ride.

The car was also holding snacks for the road.

All the heifers and skinny Sooz (thirty-six pounds at six years of age) needed nourishment.

And as I have said before, when you see grass, you pull over and eat.

Everyone also carried a sweater.

Nine hundred degrees in a non-air-conditioned car, but you needed the just-in-case sweater.

And they wondered why I vomited.

The next car that I remember so vividly was a '52 maroon (no such nomenclature as plum) Dodge, which was affectionately referred to as Betsy.

My father sure knew how to pick them.

Betsy could be relied upon in temperate weather.

Her best performances were in fall and spring.

Summer was her worst season. She overheated often, and taking her out in the heat was risky business.

She was also uncooperative in the winter.

This was unless you liked spinning around and around and around.

And there were no seatbelts.

Sometimes it was hours before you realized that you had lost one of your passengers.

Oh well, more room for everybody.

Two of the cars, Betsy and the new black Bonneville, were smokers.

I guess you could say they were excessive smokers.

My favorite experience, and I was already grown, was when the Bonneville started to smoke in the Brooklyn Battery Tunnel.

And my mother's cliché was always "helpful"—"Too bad that we don't have marshmallows," she'd announce.

The best, however, was when she added that they were old enough to smoke.

When we sold the car, let it be public knowledge, and no longer a well-kept secret, that on the way to the buyer's house, the car OD'd on smoke.

Don't quite know how, but sold it anyway.

Of course for a week after we sold it, we never picked up the phone.

Today it is a different time.

The process of buying cars has some of the same characteristics, only there are so many more gadgets, and cars seem to be made to wear out more quickly.

The basics are taken for granted.

We worried about the engine, tires, steering, heater, plugs, radiator, gas mileage, and radio (ten or twenty stations).

Today the cars come with at least four manuals to explain how the car works.

The process of buying a car is a traumatic experience!

Now you take my husband, David (and you take him, as the brilliant Henny Youngman said).

He reads a million reviews from a million different sources.

With the Internet, you can even get testimonials from satisfied and dissatisfied customers.

Then he goes to an innumerable number of dealerships (this is called comparative shopping, or trying to get as many salesmen to jump out of their windows in the shortest period of time).

He gets into the car, moves the seat, sits a while, and then meets with the salesperson.

I accompany him for the first one or two go-arounds, but after that I have had it.

I don't give a damn what he buys as long as he is happy.

My happiness depends only on whether or not my herniated discs are happy in the passenger seat.

Then he begins his test drives.

This is not over until he has come home to obsess over the three or four that he has narrowed it down to.

Finally the big day has arrived.

He waits for his salesperson, who has become pale, hunched over, and much too thin to give him "the very best deal" before he walks.

The salesperson goes into the back, meets with his manager (wrong), and comes back with the David deal.

Yes, yesterday he became the new father of a gorgeous dark "plum" (maroon) Avalon.

He will do his homework over the weekend and read the four manuals that will teach him what the hell he has in the car.

Brava!

Love,
Dr. Piggy

From: Mandel, Dr. Ellen
Sent: Wednesday, January 14, 2014, 10:22 a.m.
To: Maxam, Dr. Susan L.
Subject: Not minding one's own business

Susannah and I went to visit Aunt Sooz in Cranford—a real treat!

We stopped at her apartment briefly and drove to neighboring Westfield to do some serious shopping—so vacuous of us, and what fun.

Car was parked, got out of the car, and saw two little doggies running around the lot like bats out of hell!

No owners around!

Another couple observing the doggies too was amazed that the doggies were on their own.

A small meeting among us all led to our joining forces.

Meanwhile, these critters were trying real hard to get themselves killed by running in between cars and throwing caution to the wind.

One gentleman noted that there was a gray van with its door opened a little.

We all decided that doggie one, and his partner, doggie two, must have joined forces and squeezed through the crack!

What to do?

We coaxed the two doggies (quite a sight, watching this maneuver) into the van and closed the door.

It wasn't until we were on the way to the shoe store that we thought about the owner of the van getting into the van and finding two dogs that weren't his or hers.

Couldn't dwell on it too long because we were shopping with a store credit, the most dangerous action for two professional shoppers, and Aunt Sooz, the nonshopper whom we rehabilitate when she is with us.

We'll take this this, this, this, and this.

Enough said. We far exceeded our credit.

Probably everyone's credit, and convinced Aunt Sooz to consider a three-hundred-dollar necklace that she would have bought only if it were three dollars.

In the middle of the shopping frenzy, Susannah gets a call from the school nurse.

Matthew, the hypochondriac, is nauseous (this happens frequently).

He is pale (he is always pale)—blah, blah, blah.

He thinks he has to vomit.

Susannah gets Matthew on the phone and announces, "Guess you are too sick to go to karate."

He thinks he is going to get better.

"Have the nurse call me if you vomit," Susannah continues, and the conversation draws to a close.

Some things are just timeless.

Schoolkids have been threatening to vomit through the ages!

Back to the parking lot, after we pay the war debt in the store. The proprietor can't take the smile off of her face as she invites us to return soon.

By the way Aunt Sooz may very well return for the three-hundred-dollar necklace.

Susannah and I must have done some number on her.

Back at the parking lot, no van, no doggies.

We hope that is a good sign!

This was a great day and really took my mind off of mosquitos, malaria, and tsunamis.

Hurrah for vacuous!

Love u,
Dr. Piggy

From: Mandel, Dr. Ellen
Sent: Monday, June 2, 2014, 4:07 p.m.
To: Maxam, Dr. Susan L.
Subject: The shopaholics return, or put a muzzle on Jake

There was no way in hell that Susannah and I weren't going back to Foxes the next day to pay for our "great buys."

My son-in-law was not overjoyed to watch the two boys (even though they are in fact his), so we had to take Jacob (you remember him—the one who will report to the parole officer) with us.

He was promised new sneakers first.

My sister reported to us, not that long ago, that her oldest grandson, Daniel, aged twelve, got sneakers costing a hundred smackers (quite a contrast from my five-ninety-nine Keds at Thom McAn).

I wasn't surprised when Jacob's sneakers, which actually lit up while he walked, were seventy dollars and change.

My little spendthrift bought him two pairs, one in black and the other in navy with red lights. To up the ante, she bought each boy pool shoes, as requested by the nine-thousand-dollar day camp.

Jacob was over the moon, and he was very involved with them while we shopped.

Two hours later we knew he was a little antsy when he started to make silly faces and noises while looking at himself in the mirror.

We took him to a different neighborhood—the lower level of the store—where they carried shoes and bags.

With bunions, an inoperable cyst on the instep and plantar fasciitis, I find buying shoes is no fun.

I moved immediately to purses (known in my time as pocketbooks).

With that, Susannah's husband calls, and Jacob so wants to speak to his daddy.

All the shoppers around us are tuned in to Jacob's conversation with papa.

"Yes, Daddy, we are having so much fun. Mommy first bought me black sneakers with yellow lights for seventy dollars. Yes, that's right! And she thought they were so cool that she bought me another pair also for seventy dollars with red lights. No, she's not crazy, Daddy."

The women are now yelling at Susannah to get him off the phone.

One woman interrupts: "Put a muzzle on that kid immediately."

Then we hear, "Daddy, you haven't heard the best news. Matthew and I got wonderful pool shoes. I don't know how much they are, but they must cost a lot because they are so cool."

And finally Jacob exclaims, "Daddy isn't on the phone anymore."

All the bargain shoppers offer to house Susannah for a week or two!

Love,
Dr. Piggy

From: Mandel, Dr. Ellen
Sent: Friday, June 27, 2014, 4:33 p.m.
To: Maxam, Dr. Susan L.
Subject: The clumsy gene

My grandsons Matthew and "Wild Jake" continue to blossom and thrive.

Oh how I love to watch them interact (both good and bad).

The genetic component is fascinating.

Matthew was telling Jacob, a few days ago, how he is just like Nan—clumsy, clumsy, clumsy.

When Jake asked his brother for the definition of "clumsy," Matthew gave him an operational one.

"Remember when Nan fell down the stairs and then got up and tripped on your dinosaur? That's clumsy."

They should have known my mother and father if they wanted an operational definition.

Every time Dad cried, "Oh no," we ran for the broom or vacuum or stretcher.

More genes at work—Jake arrived needier and more in need of verbal praise.

He started to put on his shoes after breakfast, run down to the garage, hop into the car, and seatbelt himself.

He would ask his mother each time, "Are you proud of me, Mommy?" And Susannah would invariably reply, "I am so proud of you, Jacob."

Now this little ritual did not sit well with Matthew, the unneedy pragmatist.

"What is so great about putting your seatbelt on? What's to be proud of anyway?"

Matthew was given a "look" from his mama, and he discontinued his pronouncements.

Different children, different needs!

My baby Susannah turned forty on June 18. She had a number of small but wonderful celebrations. These cost her father and me big bucks. We are her gift that never stops giving.

Let me just warn you about your offspring.

When they mention the word *spa* make believe you can't hear them, or run for the hills.

No matter how much green tea and organic everything else you are offered, none of it makes up for the cost of each treatment. And if you buy the "fountain of youth serum," you can be out another $200–300.

Simply tell the vendor that you wouldn't buy it, even if Ponce de Leon were selling it.

Xxxoo,
Dr. Piggy

CHAPTER 2

PETS

To: Dr. Susan L. Maxam
Sent: Friday, December 8, 2011, 6:18 p.m.
From: Mandel, Dr. Ellen
Subject: My favorite child, Zackie the dog

My dear Dr. Wiggy,

Looking at our mantle above our fireplace in the family room, I noticed the beautiful picture of our beautiful dog Zack (short for Zaccariah) and his ashes in the beautiful urn. Whichever one of us dies last (my husband or me) will have Zackie with him or her.

We decided upon this as soon as we lost him, because he was such a precious member of our family.

I was never an animal person.

I was afraid of most garden varieties.

Our daughter was depressed when our son went away to college, so in a weak moment, my husband and I agreed to get a dog.

We needed to purchase a nonallergic dog due to the fact that my sister is a severe asthmatic.

We had seen bichons around the neighborhood, and they were adorable. Besides, I just love French pastry, so certainly that was the breed for us.

We soon learned that there was a good breeder up in the boonies about forty minutes from us.

We contacted her, and when the newest batch of puppies were but a few days old, we went up to choose our baby.

There was never a question of boy or girl when my husband heard that males were hundreds of dollars cheaper.

When we arrived at the breeder's home, we were shown to this crate housing eight little babies.

We left the selection process up to our daughter.

She picked the one who was climbing over all the others and yelping the most.

Obviously, she felt that this new brother was hyper, like the rest of us.

A perfect fit.

We waited until he was six weeks old and went back to pick him up.

He looked like Clifford instead of a petite little pup, and it was love at first sight.

Susannah held him in our son's crib blankie, and he cried all the way home. He certainly was a crybaby, but it didn't take long for him to adjust to his new family and new surroundings.

It took him a lot less time to be trained to do the pee-pee and poopie outside than it is taking my grandson to get with the program.

He was one of the sweetest, most delicious canines ever, and he was treated like any Jewish dog should be treated.

My husband bought him a daybed, and my parents never came to our house without a stuffed animal for Zackie to play with.

Although he was neutered, he still loved to do you-know-what to each stuffed animal.

Food became a bit of a problem, because like most of us in the family, he had stomach issues.

He needed special food for dogs with sensitive stomachs, and we needed a trillion dollars to buy his food. The vet didn't think he was getting enough protein, so three times a week, I made him a big boiled chicken. I had stopped cooking for my human family many years ago.

When Zackie turned one, we made him a surprise party. The invitations said "shush" on them, so that none of his friends would spill the beans.

The dogs were asked to come in costume, and they were a stitch.

While the mommies enjoyed coffee and wonderful desserts, the guests ate "frosty paws," the ice cream made for canines.

The gifts he got were sure better than the four cheese boards, three lousy fondue sets, and two umbrellas that I received at my bridal shower.

He got toys and a sweater and really great gifts.

We videotaped the party, thanks to my friend Janice, and each mother of the dog spoke for her pup like those horrible video testimonials at bar and bat mitzvahs (a personal dislike of mine).

A good time was had by all.

Our Zackie also participated in community activities such as trick or treat.

On our trips to Hilton Head each summer, we bought him a fabulous costume.

He was a witch, a bunny, a Native American in full headdress regalia, and he carried a trick-or-treat bag for goodies.

Lazy I wasn't. I took him around to all my neighbors.

They had a good laugh, Zackie had a blast, and I ate all of his candy.

Zackie, like me and his mom, fancied himself to be something of a philanthropist.

When he heard that there was an event called "Paws for Cancer," up in Bear Mountain, we signed him up and accompanied him to this worthwhile charitable event.

It wasn't fair that they had these famous TV dogs that didn't move a muscle.

They were very well poised and undaunted by the number of other animals and people.

We should have realized that Zackie was a little on the nervous side when he went into the shower when it thundered.

Anyway, we had no way of knowing that the crowds would set off his irritable bowel syndrome.

As he walked, he pooped and pooped and pooped, making it somewhat problematic for the dogs and people behind him.

Needless to say, we had to take him home, but did make a "sizable donation" to cancer.

Zackie suffered from other ailments. He had rashes and sores all over his paws. We changed his bandages every day and sometimes more often than that.

He visited Valley Cottage Animal Hospital sometimes on a weekly basis.

He never sat on the floor. He sat on his own chair right next to mine. The other animals would bark, but he waited his turn like a real "mensch."

He particularly liked having his temperature and blood pressure taken.

To each his own.

I would say that he cost us about five hundred dollars monthly.

It was what it was.

Perhaps the finest Zackie happening took place when he was five years old.

We had a workman whom we trusted do some work in our house while we were at work.

Zackie's job was to keep him company.

When I returned at noon, the worker was as white as a ghost.

"What's with the dog?" he asked me while I still had a foot out the door.

"What do you mean?" I asked in return.

"Well," he said, "the dog keeps playing the piano and then looks at me. He's been playing for over an hour.

"I called my wife," he continued, "and she says that I need a vacation.

"How long has he been playing?" the man continued.

"Since we stopped giving him tap lessons." I laughed.

Obviously, I failed to tell the poor worker that we had taught Zackie how to play the piano, and, in turn, we gave this brilliant dog a well-deserved biscuit.

When Zackie turned thirteen, we gave him a bark mitzvah.

I adored my father, and so Zackie wore my father's yarmulke and tallith.

It seemed right.

It was right.

Not long after, Zackie developed terminal cancer, and we were forced to put him to sleep.

What a loss, what emptiness.

What tears we shed.

But doesn't this reflect human life?

If a person is wonderful, the loss is profound.

Like all good things, they come to an end.

But what a gift to have relished that love and carried it in your heart forever!

Love,
Dr. Piggy

From: Mandel, Dr. Ellen
Sent: Friday, December 8, 2012, 8:00 p.m.
To: Maxam, Dr. Susan L.
Subject: Our Other Pets

Good morning, Dr. Wiggy,

I have told you all about our beloved doggie Zackie, but I never touched upon the family's other animal experiences. Let me share some of these with you.

I was never as nice to my mother as my sister, Sooz (the original Goody Two-shoes), was.

Sooz is by far the nicer person, with many fewer shtiks.

I was always cooking up some plan.

The whole family took very few vacations, but on occasion, we did.

On this particular long weekend, we traveled to a motel in Connecticut called Huckleberry Hill by all except Pop-Pop, who called it Cranberry Lane (another whole story).

On the first day, I befriended five newborn kittens.

Oh, by the way, I had just turned five.

I knew that my mommy disliked and was afraid of pussycats.

I thought she would really love it if I surprised her, and I did.

One morning after Daddy had already gotten up and Mommy was sound asleep, I put all five kittens in bed with Mommy.

Didn't take long until the kittens all began to lick Mommy's face.

She woke up and started to scream.

Daddy came flying in, and, well, I couldn't sit for a week.

Susannah had to wait until she was depressed enough to get a dog to cheer her up.

That was when she was fifteen.

Prior to that, we agreed to a hamster (who knew that was in the rat family?).

The cage was gorgeous, the expensive gravel and little toys gorgeous, and the animal god-awful ugly! Susannah cried bitterly until we bought his wheel and swing for him to exercise on.

The first night of the wheel, Susannah, who slept like a dead body, was fine, but David and I heard the goddamn hamster exercising all night.

Nobody informed us that hamsters are nocturnal.

Susannah swore that she would be the sole caregiver.

She did next to nothing, while David and I did it all.

We were sure good at teaching responsibility.

All went well until the hamster got sick.

Susannah was very savvy and diagnosed the hamster as having wet tail.

We put him in a shoebox and waited our turn to be seen at the vet.

Prognosis poor.

We brought him home and fed him through an eyedropper, but after three days he passed.

I cried. Why? I could never figure it out.

After the hamster died, the kids convinced us that they were pet deprived and guilted us into buying a beautiful bird, whom Susannah named Sunny. As always, they promised to take full charge of his grooming and training. Why did we continuously believe them? Maybe because we wanted to, or, more likely, we were brain-dead.

It didn't take but a day or two to discover that we should have called Sunny "angry bird."

He didn't' like his accommodations, his toys, or his food.

Mostly, he hated us.

When he came out of his cage on his gold-crusted stick he couldn't wait to bite us all.

A real find.

Then again you don't always get to pick your children's character traits.

Well after about three months, the bird told us in his own words that he was feeling "peckish" {ha, ha}

David was chosen to take him to the vet.

Upon arrival at the vet David waited his turn.

David called me during the visit, to tell me that things were not looking good.

The bird had something wrong with his throat.

About ten minutes later, I get a call from the vet.

He is very agitated he said, sounding concerned.

The bird, I asked. "No said the doctor, your husband."

He became faint when he saw the needle the bird was getting.

He continued to say that my husband was sitting with his head in between his knees.

A good twenty minutes passed and the phone rang.

Unfortunately he said, he just expired.

My husband I shouted.

"No," said the doctor, "the bird."

All my love,
Dr. Piggy

CHAPTER 3

Children and Grandchildren

From: Mandel, Dr. Ellen
Sent: Friday, December 1, 2011, 2:00 a.m.
To: Maxam, Dr. Susan L.
Subject: Spoiled child stays at Oneonta

Dear Dr. Wiggy,

Had a few spare minutes, and while I was looking outside at the snow, I thought about our trip to Oneonta.

Susannah attended Rockland Community College directly after high school.

She did beautifully for one and a half years, but decided that she wanted to transfer to Oneonta to be with her boyfriend.

I still cannot figure out why we agreed to this unbelievably stupid idea! But then, if I had a dollar for every stupid idea I have had, I could have retired years ago.

The college kids in those days packed their belongings in tremendous green garbage bags.

Susannah felt obliged to take all of her worldly possessions with her, and so my poor husband packed the car with what must have been twenty bags. We took our little princess up to school for checking-in day.

The morning was cold, damp, and full of emotion.

Not since Susannah had gone to summer camp and hated it had we had her away from us.

As we headed north, it began to snow lightly.

Two and a half hours later, the caravan arrived.

David schlepped the twenty garbage bags up two flights of stairs so our little darling could settle in.

No sooner had the last bag been strewn across her bed than Susannah started to cry and announced that the room smelled, and she couldn't possibly stay here.

She wanted to go home!

Not wanting to upset our little bargain more, David and I announced that we would be willing to get her a private room, but she must give it a try.

By this time, the snow had picked up.

David dragged the twenty bags downstairs with Susannah and me at his heels.

We proceeded to the housing building, where we found about thirty people ahead of us.

Maybe they all hated their rooms.

The snow picked up some more, and the veins in my neck started to protrude.

I ran up to the front of the line, explained that I was going to kill the cute little girl standing next to me, and this dean had mercy on me and took us right away.

We got Susannah a private, sweet-smelling room.

As soon as David had dropped the twentieth bag in Susannah's room, we said our good-byes and were off in what now was a blizzard.

As soon as we hit Route 17, our car took on a life of its own.

It was as if it had been placed on skates.

David, carpal tunnel and all, had his hands clenched to the steering wheel.

Seven and a half hours later, David literally peeled his hands off of the wheel as we arrived in our driveway.

We had already decided that we didn't want to see our second-born until summer.

Matters were made worse when the garage door wouldn't open and we didn't have our keys.

Keep in mind that it was still snowing.

David ran across the street to our neighbors and borrowed a ladder.

He ran around back and placed it near our kitchen window. One, two, and down he fell into a pile of snow.

Don't laugh, but hard not to.

On the second try, success.

David opened the window, and, carrying a foot of snow with him, climbed into the kitchen, just in time to answer the phone, which was ringing and ringing.

It was none other than the crying Susannah, who announced that she hated the school and wanted us to pick her up.

David announced that even if she died during the night, we weren't coming for her.

A good time was had by all.

Love,
Dr. Piggy

From: Mandel, Dr. Ellen
Sent: Friday, December 9, 2011, 10:47 a.m.
To: Maxam, Dr. Susan L.
Subject: Take out my adenoids instead

Dear Dr. Wiggy,

Yesterday was my grandson Jacob's adenoidectomy, and a horrible time was had by all.

My job assignment was given to me, in great detail, as early as last week.

My role was to accompany Susannah and Sam to make Susannah as nuts as I was.

Mission accomplished.

Because I was giving the beginning of my oral finals all day today, I decided to take my own car and to leave early to be on time, and to get into as much traffic as possible.

Jacob—or patient, as it was—woke up in the morning crying.

He wanted to begin crying before the day hardly began.

When he found that he couldn't have his milk, he was inconsolable.

I like to arrive at the hospital as early as possible because I can't take the anxiety that accompanies being late.

I like to get to my destination a half hour early to have that additional cup of coffee that will bring on my acid reflux earlier and permit me to work myself up to a crescendo of hysteria.

I suggested to my son-in-law that he leave himself enough traveling time.

As usual, he didn't listen, and they all arrived five minutes late.

Jacob must have remembered his milk upon entering the hospital, so he gave a crying version of "Am I Blue."

My job at this crossroads was to calm Jacob down while Susannah and Sam filled out the appropriate papers.

By this time it was 11:00 a.m. with surgery scheduled for 12:00.

I volunteered to take Jacob's place, and I am sure that they would have taken me were it not for the fact that I had my adenoids and tonsils removed when I was eight.

One of the many props that I brought with me were candy canes with reindeer pipe cleaners and eyes.

The "creative me" planned to make reindeer bracelets with Jacob.

Somehow, dunderhead me didn't realize that Jacob would notice only the candy canes.

When he was told that he couldn't eat them, or anything else, he showed his gratitude by turning his crying into shrieking.

Susannah at first didn't know how to thank me, but I remember hearing the words *moron* and the like (she later apologized).

Jacob's name was finally called, and we all proceeded with Buzz Lightyear, coat bags, and so forth, to the next waiting room.

About an hour later, the doctor came out to report that Jacob and Buzz Lightyear were doing well. Operation a success!

Xxxooo,
Dr. Piggy

From: Mandel, Dr. Ellen
Sent: Monday, December 26, 2011, 7:57 p.m.
To: Maxam, Dr. Susan L.
Subject: Will he poop on the potty before he is married?

My dear Dr. Wiggy,

I am so happy that Chanukah is drawing to a close. I look very much like the traditional latke (potato pancake).

These little suckers are fried in oil until crispy, and when they arrive from their plate to your mouth, it is a gastronomic experience unlike any other.

They also provide for an entire week of calories on many of the new diets that are out there.

I must tell you that last week was as thrilling as the Fourth of July, Christmas, and Easter combined.

Last week was the celebration of celebrations!

My three-year-and-one-month-old grandson agreed (and the key word here is "agreed") to make poopie on the potty.

This was a far cry from the toilet training of yesteryear.

Right before my son and daughter turned two, respectively, they were introduced to the potty and told that this was where they would be making.

It took a little work on my part, but my efforts paid off.

I put their little tushies on the potty after breakfast, lunch, and dinner and read to them while they sat there and finally did their business. My son was rewarded with gum and my daughter with M&Ms.

Using this older-than-old primary reinforcement technique, they were trained within a week or so.

Of course there were accidents, but they soon learned like millions before them learned.

Today, mama waits until the child is ready.

Some children aren't ever ready, so that their husbands and wives do the training.

The process now is one where the child is in charge.

The process then becomes one of serious negotiation.

The child can provide a list of expensive toys that will be his if he agrees (another important word) to place his tushie, like millions before him, on the potty.)

For some children bribery doesn't work at all.

They simply announce that they can, but choose not to make on their potties.

Some bring their own Pull-ups to Mama after the fact, while others get as far as the bathroom and then make in their diaper or Pull-up.

Now that all physical interaction is forbidden and reported to be "child abuse," my method of smacking the kid in the head is taboo.

Hence these very bright toddlers dictate to their not-as-bright parents.

I still prefer my method. What about you?

Hope you are doing well.

I will write again soon.

Love xxxxoooo,
Dr. Piggy

From: Mandel, Dr. Ellen
Sent: Saturday, February 11, 2012 7:50 a.m.
To: Maxam, Dr. Susan L.
Subject: Scream and Shout

Good morning,

Tomorrow is Matthew's sixth birthday party, at a place called Scream and Shout.

There is no doubt in my mind why it was given that name.

It could be shortened to just scream to be more fitting.

When did the small at-home parties for kids become passé?

I remember baking cupcakes with my mother for my party.

Maybe twelve friends attended, and everyone had cake, ice cream, and soda.

Everyone opened presents (small, inexpensive gifts), you played pin the tail on the donkey or turkey or whatever farm animal was available, musical chairs, and everyone went bye-bye.

I should have realized that things were changing when my own kids went to bar and bat mitzvahs. Parents signed up for a place three years in advance. The kids even received save-the-date cards.

I didn't know what the kids were doing next week, and now we all had to commit to a date three years from Saturday. People started losing their minds and their perspective at that time.

Two good examples in point, come to mind.

Actually, they blew my mind.

One woman had booked a country club near us for her son's bar mitzvah.

She objected to the curtains and chair coverings.

What to do?

Crisis.

She solved her so-called problem by paying to redo all the curtains and chair coverings. Nuts? Oh yes, nuts.

Then there was the mom who wanted the invitations to be wowers.

She made shirt-size invitations that were delivered to all the guests' houses in big shirt boxes.

Take this money and give it to charity, I thought.

Therefore, these kids' parties are not unexpected in this day and age.

It's nice that these moms and dads who are twenty years or more past their bar mitzvahs still believe in conspicuous consumption.

Kids are permitted to invite seventy-five of their closest friends to their party. "Closest" means that they have spoken to these kids at least twice.

Themes are a must.

We just had the birthday theme.

Themes today for kids include Thomas, Nemo, Toy Story, Spiderman, and the like.

Clowns, magicians, roller skaters, and dancing monkeys are hired at exorbitant prices to make the kids laugh.

My mother didn't care who laughed. You came, ate, and left.

If you didn't have a good time, it was your own damn fault. Then don't come next time.

It was that simple.

So, my dear Matthew, in spite of your nanny's observations, have a wonderful sixth birthday at Scream and Scream and Scream.

I only hope that grandpa and I can be at next year's extravaganza.

Love,
Dr. Piggy

From: Mandel, Dr. Ellen
Sent: February 13, 2012, 8:00 a.m.
To: Maxam, Dr. Susan L.
Subject: Mathew's sixth birthday, part two

Tonight we are all going to the Cheesecake Factory to celebrate the second part of our grandson Matthew's sixth birthday.

Not unlike a true bar mitzvah, this has two parts.

Last week's party was at that "Scream and Scream," or whatever, that I told you about.

Tonight is most of the immediate family.

(Our son Leigh lives in Miami.)

Matthew called his nanny this morning (that would be me, nanny) to ask if as a special treat, I could bring him and his brother pancakes and sausage from McDonald's.

Out the door I flew, to fill out this request.

Good that we don't make him omnipotent or too special.

After thanking me, which is always refreshing, he announced that his daddy let him pick the Cheesecake Factory.

I asked him why that was his choice, and in a matter-of-fact way, he told me that he loved their sliders and particularly the waiters all coming over with a cake and candles and singing "Happy Birthday" to the birthday person, and even clapping.

He has my humbleness and lack of pretentiousness, along with the keen characteristic of not wanting to be the center of attention.

Is he lucky or not?

Oh, well, the Cheesecake Factory is always good for a perpetual dieter like me.

It is hard to consume fewer than five thousand calories at one sitting.

There are other perks.

There is an ambulance parked directly outside the restaurant for free pickups and deliveries to the ICU cardiac unit at Nyack Hospital.

Love you,
Dr. Piggy

From: Mandel, Dr. Ellen
Sent: Friday, March 16, 2012, 9:59 p.m.
To: Maxam, Dr. Susan L.
Subject: The demolition squad strikes again

Good evening, Dr. Wiggy,

The demolition squad, better known as my grandsons, just left my house after a wonderful St. Patrick's Day repast. No, it is not confusing to them.

Even though we are practicing Jews, we all love to learn about other religions, cultures, and traditions.

This is a good lesson to teach young children to respect everyone!

My husband, the fabulous gourmet chef (I only poison people), whipped up a mean corned beef and cabbage with boiled potatoes and topped off by my dear friend Anna's (the owner of the best bakery in the world, Anna's Bakery) Irish soda bread, hot cross buns, and shamrock cookies.

A little bit of heaven!

What is it about grandchildren that makes our hearts sing? I certainly don't love them any more than I do my children.

That would be impossible.

What makes this love so different and so special? As a professional worrier, it isn't that I worry less about them. It's not that it's easier to watch them,

Au contraire.

It is more taxing because we are older, more tired, and perhaps less patient.

So what's this miracle that makes our hearts sing?

What is it that makes me put my coat on and fly out the door in search of Lego Space Police and Spanish Buzz Lightyear from *Toy Story*?

What is it that makes me turn all my ready cash into stickers?

What was it this evening that prevented my husband from killing our three-year-old grandson when he accidentally broke a very expensive Chinese jug in our living room?

Our own children would have been seriously maimed.

My husband's answer to this question was a wise one.

The miracle of our love for our grandchildren remains with the love we had and have for our children. It brings us back to our youth and to theirs as well. We were so awed by the love we had for our babies.

The difference with our grandchildren is that the weight of responsibility, of self-evaluation, of what we did or what we said, is very much lifted from our shoulders. This frees us, in a sense, along with the freedom of financial responsibility and often the luxury of having more time.

And, from my perspective, the fact that this is God's gift to us makes it the most precious and special kind of love.

On a lighter note, ninety is looking good as far as my retirement goes, so I can afford all the Legos and Buzz Lightyears.

Much love,
An exhausted Dr. Piggy

From: Mandel, Dr. Ellen
Sent: Sunday, April 15, 2012, 1:27 p.m.
To: Maxam, Dr. Susan L.
Subject: Pounds for Pesach

My dear Dr. Wiggy,

So nice having heard from you.

We are taking the kids and grandkids once again to the Cheesecake Factory tonight, because we are afraid that we haven't piled on enough pounds for Pesach (Passover).

Isn't that a great name for a new foundation, "Pounds for Pesach" (Passover)?

The little guy is improving his behavior, and we may not have to deal with his probation officer when he grows up.

He will be three and a half next month, on my birthday actually, and he is still afraid to make poopie on the potty.

I once again have been forbidden by my daughter to mention the topic to her.

He now says that he will go when he is tall.

Considering that he is only in the twenty-fifth percentile in his age group for height, well you do the math—nineteen, twenty—who knows?

Xxxooo,
Dr. Piggy

From: Mandel, Dr. Ellen
Sent: November 28, 2012, 3:00 p.m.
To: Maxam, Dr. Susan L.
Subject: Susannah refused to be cultured

Good evening, Dr. Wiggy,

Thanks for the beautiful thank-you note.

You deserve such wonderful things, because you are so very special.

David lost the toss of the coin and had to take Leigh to the airport.

Leigh usually does not take much of a liking to young children, but his nephews are getting older, and he seemed to enjoy playing with them. Leigh made up this ridiculous game called Monster Worm, and the kids were crazy about the game and their uncle Leigh.

I spoke to Leigh this morning (he is back home in Florida), and I inquired if he wanted to come in again for Chanukah. He announced that he had enough Monster Worm to last till spring.

One of the discussions over the holiday was exposing kids to enough culture these days.

If the activity doesn't start with the letter *i* as in iPhone, iPad, iPod, the activity isn't well received.

The i's are taking the place of babysitters all over the country.

You can leave your kid in the evening and find him in the same place the next morning, still playing with his iPad.

My kids were exposed to culture.

My Susannah refused to get with the program, from her earliest years.

This was very disconcerting to her parents, so we introduced her to one thing after another, hoping that one area would appeal to her very mature tastes.

One of the offerings was piano.

Susannah was placed under the tutelage of a very well-known piano teacher in New City, New York.

She had a passion for her music, but not for my Susannah.

There might have been some reasons for this.

Susannah never practiced and never improved. She was, however, still included in the yearly recital.

You know the now-common "no child left behind."

Well, in this case, it would have been better to leave this child behind.

The day of the recital Susannah looked beautiful.

Her little song might have been better received, if she didn't blow bubbles with her gum during the last and most important part of her performance.

She didn't get rave reviews from bursting out in laughter when the other kids made mistakes either. We were so proud!

The day after her performance (her flowers hadn't even had a chance to wither), her teacher called to announce that Susannah was unteachable.

I can't remember how long she was grounded for.

It was a long time until she was reintroduced to culture.

Love,
Dr. Piggy

From: Mandel, Dr. Ellen
Sent: Friday, July 8, 2014, 6:41 p.m.
To: Maxam, Dr. Susan L.
Subject: A day at the museum (or how to be put down by an eight-year-old)

Talking about gifted (not a bad segue, huh?), on Sunday, we took our grandson Matthew to the Museum of Natural History, primarily to see the dinosaurs. Jake was left home until he could appreciate the experience more.

I wish they had left me home, until I could appreciate it more!

Don't misunderstand me, I do enjoy some of the exhibits like the crown jewels (wrong museum), and the like, but I like to look at all the sauruses (tyran, bronco, ptery) and not linger.

Matthew and David read every fact about every dinosaur and its mother and all its relatives on both sides!

They weren't alone.

Natives and tourists looked up and down and sideways and around and took thousands of pictures and then looked some more, and I said to myself, enough already.

How long can you look at these creatures, and what the hell are you going to do with all those pictures?

The one time I did open my mouth, I put my big foot in it.

There was a very nice picture of the pterosaurs dropping food down into their babies' mouths.

"Look at that," I said enthusiastically.

"The mommy is taking such good care of her little babies."

Didn't take more than a minute for Matthew to tap me on the shoulder and say in a voice loud enough for the spectators to hear, "Nan, you're wrong. If you had read the next paragraph, you would have learned that the picture was false. The babies didn't really need help. They wanted to be totally independent, and their mothers did not feed them. The artist was incorrect."

"Oh, what good news," I replied, while the nosy spectators chuckled.

I can make an idiot out of myself without having an eight-year-old do it for me!

I did a little better with the African mammals, many of whom had a strong resemblance to some of my grandfather's relatives on my mother's side.

You know, big, bulky, a little confused looking.

I read most of the blurbs under them.

The only problem I had was the leopard pushpig. As Matthew explained, there was a space between leopard and pushpig, and he pointed out the leopard and in the background the pushpig.

Maybe I will do better with the planetarium.

And Jake is coming with me.

I am not taking this by myself!

All my love,
Dr. Piggy

CHAPTER 4

Calamity Jane

From: Mandel, Dr. Ellen
Sent: Sunday, February 19, 2012, 9:44 a.m.
To: Maxam, Dr. Susan L.
Subject: IBM, here I come

Good morning, Dr. Wiggy,

The dust has settled from my pneumonia and David's angioplasty.

At sixty-six, we are truly the walking wounded.

I remember the days when I had more energy.

My sister insists, however that she and I (frequently referred to by too many of my students as me and her) do more in one day than most people do in a week.

I was thinking about how many jobs I juggled at once back then.

At Pace, in the early eighties, many of us served on the IBM Business Communication Team.

We provided upper-level management with a short business course in business communication.

On this particular morning in August, for the first time in my entire life, I overslept.

I was the benchmark speaker, and I was expected to be in Briarcliff, New York, early in the morning.

I gave myself what my mother would call "a cat's wash," dressed, and ran out the door to get over the Tappan Zee Bridge.

(That by the way is the bridge where it is necessary to wear your shower cap each day as you drive over, because you could end up in the Hudson River at any time.) In any case, when I was sitting in traffic, I looked in my rearview mirror only to notice that I had no make-up on and looked disgusting.

I made up my mind that when I arrived at the traffic light at the Marble Avenue Exit of the Saw Mill Parkway (since the light has never been green in the thirty-five years that I have arrived there), I would put on a little lipstick.

I always carried an emergency lipstick in my bag, and this sure was an emergency.

On schedule I arrived at the light and reached into my bag for my trusty lipstick.

My window was open and a guy in a small red car was looking over in my direction.

In the blink of an eye, and worried that the light would turn green, I applied my lipstick.

When I looked in the mirror to blot, I realized to my horror, that I had applied my mascara.

My lips were totally black.

The man in the car on the side of me was laughing hysterically.

"I can't wait to tell my wife," he told me.

"I don't give a damn what you tell your wife," I snarled and pulled over to the shoulder.

For ten minutes, I tried desperately to get rid of the black.

There was still black after those few minutes, but now my lips were also red and puffy.

I arrived at IBM and used the story as my opening attention getter.

My first topic for the morning was "speaker anxiety," so I certainly had adequate material.

That's my story for this morning, and I am sticking to it.

Much love,
Xxxxoooo,
Dr. Piggy

From: Mandel, Dr. Ellen
Sent: Monday, March 20, 2012, 8:34 p.m.
To: Maxam, Dr. Susan L.
Subject: Whose funeral is it anyway?

My dear Dr. Wiggy,

I wanted to thank you in advance for writing what I am sure will be a spectacular nomination for me. I was speaking to my sister this morning to merely say hi. (We speak many times a day and never run out of things to say. I am truly blessed.)

Anyway she told me that she attended her colleague's father's funeral and then began laughing hysterically.

Now our group is bizarre (not helped by our grandparents being first cousins), but this was not a usual reaction to such a sad event.

When questioned, she explained the following.

The deceased was Roy Wood.

Every time the rabbi referred to him in his eulogy, he called him Roy Rogers.

After three or four times, my sister had trouble keeping it together.

This reminds me of my own funeral mishap.

Our friend and neighbor across the street lost his dad.

There was no doubt that, out of respect, I would attend the services.

The service conflicted with my work, so I told him that I would meet him and his wife at the cemetery.

He asked me to meet him and the family at 11:30 a.m. in front of the cemetery office.

Since I couldn't find my way out of a paper bag, I left extra time to get there.

I arrived at 11:20 a.m. and immediately saw some of the mourners on the steps leading to the office.

I hadn't realized that my friend had such a big, big family.

Now, I have always been a crier, and when I saw some of my friend's relatives crying, I began to wail.

What a wonderful person, said one.

So charitable, said another.

By this time I had used up all my tissues, and my face had turned beet red like it always does when I cry.

The third relative added that she was such a good mother.

"Mother," I said. "You mean father."

"Listen," she said. "Molly was a wonderful mother."

How was I supposed to know that this wasn't my friend's family!

All those tears, and I didn't even know the woman.

I was a little early and as luck would have it, this was not the right group, and it was the burial right before my friend's father's.

I cried with the "right group" when they arrived.

And from that time on, I ask for the family name before I make that mistake again.

Well, my dear Dr. Wiggy, it is past my bedtime.

Love xxxxooo,
Your old friend and admirer,
Dr. Piggy

From: Mandel, Dr. Ellen
Sent: March 28, 2012, 8:35 a.m.
To: Maxam, Dr. Susan L.
Subject: There are no nice bees.

I don't have to worry about cataract surgery on Wednesday, because I failed the stress test yesterday at my preop visit to my internist/cardiologist.

I can continue using my Seeing Eye dog for the time being.

Last week when I was driving at night, I ended up on my neighbor's lawn.

What a surprise for both of us!

We were both surprised and indignant that my car and I were perched in the middle of his shrubs! This was entirely different from the time that I called David from a tree not far away from my home.

That was almost not my fault at all.

Two bees flew into my window, and no matter how I insisted that they leave, they wouldn't.

When I tried to swat them, I lost control of the car and ended up in the branches, unable to extricate myself, but nevertheless free of the bees.

Bees cannot be trusted.

Perhaps they are much like my driving—not to be trusted.

When we still lived on Ocean Parkway in Brooklyn, we decided to take the kids to Great Adventure.

Leigh was four and Susannah one.

We walked out to our car and saw a large bee swarming around us.

The good advice that my mother gave me was given to the children.

"Don't worry," I told them. "Stand still and they won't bother you. They are more afraid of you than you are of them."

Wrong, wrong, wrong.

That bee was so frightened, he stung me with a vengeance.

I traveled to Great Adventure with an ice pack on my chest!
New advice to my kids—
When you see a bee, run for your lives.

Xxxooo,
Dr. Piggy

From: Mandel, Dr. Ellen
Sent: Thursday, April 19, 2012, 8:05 p.m.
To: Maxam, Dr. Susan L.
Subject: The blush-brush mystery

My dear Dr. Wiggy,

Wanted to touch base with you tonight because tomorrow will be a magical day.

So thrilled that you are being honored.

Call me Saturday, and tell me lots of details.

I was reminiscing this morning—who knows why—and thought I would share a funny story with you.

I was thinking how oblivious to detail I have always been.

You know, wearing cleaning tickets and labels, clothes inside out, mismatched pants and sweaters, two different shoes, open-toe shoes with flowers sticking out of the toe (picked up inadvertently in the parking lot of Pace), and I could go on and on.

But this little mishap was one for the books.

About twenty years ago, when I stopped rubbing lipstick into my cheeks (a la my nanny), I invested in some blush and a rather pricey blush brush that the saleswoman in the cosmetics department of Lord and Taylor convinced me that I just had to have.

I carried both items in my purse, in case I had to look magnificent immediately.

After about three or four days, the blush brush vanished.

I checked the obvious places—refrig, stove—and it was nowhere to be found.

I must admit that I was enjoying using it, so after a few more days, I purchased another one.

Although no one offered me a movie contract because of my new look, I was enjoying my purchase for the next month or so.

Then as before, no blush brush.

Accidents happen, I told myself, though I really don't recall my leaving it anywhere.

After about a week, I bought another one and placed it at the bottom of my purse so that it couldn't fall out of the purse somehow, and I checked often to make sure that it was still with me.

After the next loss of brush, I decided that I was losing my mind, and, frankly, I was frightened.

But I still went back to the same woman at Lord and Taylor.

She was no doubt preparing for a trip to Hawaii, after making a fortune in commissions from the customer who obviously had a blush-brush fetish.

It was on a day when my son returned from college when I lost my brush for the last time.

As I sat with him on my bed, he took my bag and commented on how heavy it was.

I had noticed that for a few days, but had thought that it was because of all the junk I was carrying.

My son emptied the bag and searched the inside.

It was then that he discovered the hole in the lining, and when he searched further, he opened up the lining just a drop more and all the blush brushes fell onto my bed.

My son could not stop laughing, and my daughter peed in her pants.

This is a true story, and the names have not been changed to protect the guilty.

That's about it, my dear Dr. Wiggy.

Can't wait to hear from everyone about how well you spoke in retelling your story of dealing with cancer and how you are a fabulous survivor if ever there was one.

Good night!

Love,
Dr. Piggy

From: Mandel, Dr. Ellen
Sent: Wednesday, May 2, 2012, 10:30 a.m.
To: Maxam, Dr. Susan L.
Subject: A run-in with the law

My dear Dr. Wiggy,

I never told you that I have had several run-ins with the law over the years.

The first one was cake related.

One of my favorite cakes in the world happens to be chocolate brownies with a thick layer of chocolate fudge on top.

At Pace, one of the speeches that we used to require was a speech to demonstrate. Needless to say, when one of my students demonstrated how to prepare fudgy brownies, some with walnuts, and some with sprinkles, I had a real hard time concentrating on her speech while concentrating at the same time on her brownies.

By the end of her presentation, she might as well have been concluding with blah blah, blah, blah blah, because I couldn't wait for my eating orgy to begin.

I took a half at first to look like a lady, right after class, but by brownie number three, that lady façade was gone.

My mother, God rest her soul, always said that I was "dumb like a fox."

In front of the class, I announced that for our last day of class, each student, if they cared to, (you can't make cake compulsory) could bring in a sweet treat, but this student had to bring in a tray of brownies. (Her grade would not be affected by her brownies.)

Sure enough, on the last day of class, the fudgy brownies appeared.

There was a tray for the class and a tray for me to take home to my family, who have rarely seen any of the spoils for obvious reasons.

The class finally ended, and when I got into my car, I delicately pulled off the Saran Wrap and said, "Let the games begin."

I was eating and driving, and driving and eating.

I have a heavy foot, and it wasn't long before I heard the siren behind me.

The officer pulled me over.

I opened the window and reached toward my glove compartment.

The cop took one look at me and said, "Don't reach for anything. Your mouth, hands, and hair are full of fudge. You are a mess. Do not dirty your license and registration, and especially keep your hands away from me. Just go and never come back to my area here again."

So I left, filthy but happy.

No ticket and almost half a tray of brownies left.

All my love,
Dr. Piggy

From: Mandel, Dr. Ellen
Sent: Monday, May 21, 2012, 6:22 p.m.
To: Maxam, Dr. Susan L.
Subject: Who's the real bitch?

My dear, dear Dr. Wiggy,

Just came back from nonsunny Florida and brought the rain back with me.

Do you know that our friends always ask us what weeks we are taking for our vacation and then choose weeks that are nowhere near ours?

I was sure that I told you about my attending the Criminal Justice holiday party years ago, but if I haven't, here it goes.

When Michelle Newman (a French professor at Pace) had her eyes on my office and tortured me into switching, I landed in the criminal justice office with two police lieutenants and a fire marshal.

Well, when I was invited to one of their departmental holiday parties, I accepted.

On party day, I was running a little behind schedule, so I kind of tore into parking lot three.

I did, however, stop at the stop sign.

All of a sudden, this woman popped out of the bushes and verbally attacked me.

"What's the matter with you?" she yelled. "There's a stop sign."

"I stopped," I replied.

"No, you didn't, you little bitch." (At least she thought I was little.

"Go f—k yourself," I screamed back.

After the smoke stopped coming out of the top of my head, I parked my car and ran to Gottesman, where the party was being held.

It was very festive and very crowded.

A few minutes after I arrived, one of my lieutenant friends took me around and told me that he wanted me to meet the assistant DA.

The woman turned around, and who was it, the shrew from hell who called me a bitch.

You know the one I told to go f--k herself.

"Oh yes," I said.

"We've already met."

She called me a bitch, and I told her what she could go do with herself.

We both laughed.

Do you think the incident had anything to do with the fact that that was the last invite I had to the holiday party?

Nah.

Much love, my dear Dr. Wiggy.

Let me hear from you soon.

Love,
Dr. Piggy

From: Mandel, Dr. Ellen
Sent: June 28, 2012, 1:00 p.m.
To: Maxam, Dr. Susan L.
Subject: Where are you, Perry Mason?

Good afternoon, my dear Dr. Wiggy,

I am still reviewing in my mind the events of the last few days and the thrill of winning the Jefferson Award.

This is most assuredly one of my greatest accomplishments, although in my heart of hearts, I don't feel deserved of such an honor.

My second-greatest accomplishment for that evening would have to be getting rid of my torturous girdle and unbearably painful shoes.

Upon my return, my focus was upon dealing with my new iPhone, purchased during a short lapse of consciousness in the Verizon store.

On my previous phone, I managed to take a picture of myself sitting on the toilet, so what would make me think that I was ready for this upgrade?

Only rampant stupidity.

When the Verizon salesperson asked me if I cared to purchase insurance, I screamed out, "Absolutely!" (I knew my previous track record, and so there wasn't a second of hesitation.)

Yes, yes, a thousand times yes!

The bad news that came along with this, however, was that the replacement phones cost $169 without the protective covering.

Another accidental dropping of the phone in the toilet could mean near bankruptcy.

On the night that we returned from DC, I had to pick up David at his office in Englewood, New Jersey.

Before I began my trek down the Palisades, I stopped at the supermarket to buy myself a nutritious dinner—broiled chicken and a big bag of M&Ms to send the chicken down.

The phone, my keys, and my dinner were all on the front seat.

I was doing an admirable job on the M&Ms when a sense of reality took over.

You are eating a whole day's calories, according to most of the fashionable diets today, most of which I have tried, with limited or no success.

Desperation!

Decision-making time!

Be a disgusting litterbug and throw the bag out of the window, or consume another whole day of calories.

Litter, calories, calories, or litter.

The conversation with myself was short.

Shame on me. In this emergency, I flung the bag out of the window.

Another reason why I am going to hell.

As I was riding down the Palisades, I decided to call my Susannah, whom I speak to only fifty times a day.

No phone.

Pulled over to check the car, and lo and behold, phone gone.

Oh no, I thought. I must have thrown the phone out along with the chicken and the M&Ms.

Didn't take long for God to punish me for littering, now, did it?

Never heard of it taking only fifteen minutes.

When I finally got to David's office, I was beside myself.

I would have to 'fess up to my crime because I wanted to go back to look for the infamous bag.

To make a short story long, we went back to the scene of the heinous crime.

Hurrah! I saw the bag.

I jumped out of the car, hoping to find the phone, chicken, and M&Ms.

The bag was ripped, crushed, but worst of all, empty.

"Oh my God," I cried, "a bird must have eaten everything and flown off with the phone!"

You hear that all the time, don't you?

A big bird swoops up a crying child.

Is a big crow able to lift up a phone?

David and I searched the area thoroughly.

No bird near, nor talking on the phone.

Such disappointment.

David then had the first intelligent thought of the evening.

Go back to the supermarket.

David urged me to go into the store, even though the latter was about to close.

Yes, you guessed it.

It had been left by this dimwit in the cart!

Red cart, red phone.

The store manager handed me my phone, and everyone lived happily ever after.

Love you,
Dr. Piggy

From: Mandel, Dr. Ellen
Sent: Saturday, August 8, 2013, 2:25 p.m.
To: Maxam, Dr. Susan L
Subject: David elects himself president of the Decorating Committee

Dear Dr. Wiggy,

David and I are redoing our tiny bathroom off the master bathroom because the shower is corroding.

Rather than redo it completely, which was my idea (spendthrift), David decided that we were going to do "a few things" (cheapskate).

David spent months researching every tile, faucet, and towel hook.

Several salespeople committed suicide; others just ran into the back when he arrived in their showrooms.

Some tiles were too dark, some too light, some lacked continuity—whatever the crap that meant.

His reputation preceded him.

Workers told other workers about Dr. Mandel, the perfectionist.

There was also the issue of our flowered wallpaper.

I voted to take it down, because we had the tile. My vote was vetoed.

Add to the mix that David bought this horrible mosaic online.

This was handmade (I think by some blind person) and shipped to us from Israel. This was another bone of contention, because of its extreme ugliness. It was supposed to be used in the kitchen.

It was banished from the kitchen by me and placed in the depths of the basement.

It came to life, a la David, the renowned decorator, and you will never guess where it ended up.

How did you know?

It's framed in the bathroom along with the flowered paper, old mirror, old vanity, and new tiles.

Some people would say that it is eclectic.

Some other people might say what my mama would say: "ugly as sin."

Now the final thing to be purchased was a bath mat.

Size, texture, color, and durability were the variables that were considered.

After four trips to Bed Bath and Beyond, made by me, we narrowed it down.

Now it was a choice between the small or medium one.

My mission for yesterday afternoon, if I decided to take it, was to drive to Bed Bath and Beyond one more time and bring both the small and the medium home to be obsessed over.

I accepted the mission.

I arrived at Bed Bath and Beyond and got a warm greeting from all the sales associates, who knew me by face and, even worse, by name.

I quickly picked up the small and the medium mat when all of a sudden, I spotted it.

It was an adorable onesie in dark-red rich velvet with white polka dots.

"Savannah," I said aloud. Perfect for her. This is my new adopted great-niece.

Talk about obsessing (probably through association)—small or medium, medium or small.

Medium, I finally decided.

I took the two mats, small and medium, and the onesie, size medium, and approached the cashier.

"Well," I said, "I will take the two mats and this beautiful onesie for my great-niece Savannah."

"Well," the guy said with a big smile on his face, "I hope your great-niece is a dog, because that onesie is for a medium-sized dog for the holiday."

I will say no more!

Much love,
Ellen

From: Mandel, Dr. Ellen
Sent: Saturday, December 7, 2013, 8:25 p.m.
To: Maxam, Dr. Susan L.
Subject: Help at the Help Desk

My dearest Dr. VP Wiggy,

Your letter went out late this afternoon, and hopefully it will further support your finalist position.

Whatever the outcome, I am so proud of you!

This week, I had a problem with my computer.

I should mention that I always have a problem with mine, and everybody else's, computer.

But this was a problem that could be fixed only by Pace's help desk.

How did I know this?

Certainly not on my own.

Someone told me.

I should give a little background information about me and anything that involves technology. While I was taking my PhD at Columbia University (threw this in so that nobody would think that I was a total incompetent), I was banished from the videotaping room because I broke the machine trying to videotape my undergraduate students (better throw in that I was a straight-A student, lest everyone skips "idiot" and goes right to "imbecile").

Nice that that nomenclature is no longer used.

Back to the help desk. Two very bright clinicians began to ask me questions in a courageous effort to help me.

The hell with the answers. I didn't understand anything they asked after an "Are you Dr. Mandel?"

It is times like these that you want to say, "No, I am not Dr. Mandel. I am Dr. Turkey-lurkey or Dr. Henny-penny."

These are not proud moments.

I swallowed my pride, however, and announced to the two technicians that I didn't care what was wrong with it. I went on to say that I would return in twenty minutes and that I was sure that they would figure it out and fix it by then.

As I waited down the hall and out of sight, I pondered some of the terms that were so new and had a very different meaning from their past ones.

One of the Verizon technicians told me last week to delete the cookies. Cookies to me come by the pound, from my friend Anna's bakery, and are twelve dollars a pound. A cookie was also something that you put in your shoe to correct an orthopedic problem with your feet.

Hard drive was Pennsylvania Avenue in Brooklyn. It was a hard drive because of the bumpy, lumpy road. Husbands took their wives who were overdue in giving birth to Pennsylvania Avenue for a hard drive with the hope that these ladies would go into labor. Success rate unknown.

Log-in is something that men out west did when they were intending to chop down trees. (Jewish men never went loggin'.)

Twitter—closest we came was calling someone a "little twit" (not a compliment—probably a good definition is "smartass").

I could go on ad nauseam, but back to the help desk.

I came back in twenty minutes, and these two brilliant technicians had worked their magic.

The problem with all its mumbo-jumbo words was resolved.

My computer was all better and ready to go.

And that's just what I did. I went out of the help desk as fast as I could. I'll never know if the problem recurs, because I never knew what the problem was.

If it rears its ugly head, I'll just wait till someone tells me to go to the help desk.

And I will go.

Because I don't have to stay, and they won't make me cry!

Love,
Dr. Piggy

CHAPTER 5

TRAVEL

From: Mandel, Dr. Ellen
Sent: Wednesday, December 28, 2011, 4:26 p.m.
Subject: Traveling light

Dear Dr. Wiggy,

So good speaking to you today.

As I mentioned, David and I are preparing for our forthcoming trip.

One of us is behaving nicely, and one is not doing well at all.

What's your best guess as to which one I am?

I was never a good traveler, but thank God today I no longer get carsick!

One must be grateful for small favors.

Trips involve change, a certain degree of independence, and coping skills that enable one to roll with the punches.

I hate change, am very dependent, and fold with the punches.

Would you like to travel with me?

No one would.

And yet, because my husband loves traveling so much, I have always given in and thus have been fortunate enough to see the world.

Actually, it is he who tells me how fortunate I am.

The actual preparation starts weeks before.

I have to have enough time to get myself to my fevered pitch.

What shall I take with me?

I love these efficient travelers who go to Chico's and pick out four or five mix-and-match outfits that they purchase and take with them wherever they are going, whether they are staying five or fifty days.

They glide onto the plane with a tiny overnight case.

They have a certain joie de vivre, those bitches.

My husband and I use the trudging method; we are burdened with enough suitcases to move anywhere permanently.

I have wardrobes for all seasons and sizes.

When I want to visit Fantasy Land, I look over my size sixes and eights.

When I choose to be realistic, I look at the clothes that are only ten pounds away, my size tens.

If I ever want to actually fit into my frocks, I pack my twelves.

Even if we are going to the tropics, I take several sweaters a la my nanny, who insisted that we would either be cold or catch pneumonia wherever we went.

Our medication alone needs its own suitcase. Who the heck ever said better safe than sorry?

Too bad that I take this so literally.

Although only once did I take medication for bubonic plague (only kidding).

What amazes me the most, however, is that although I have taken thousands of pounds with me, I always forget something important like a toothbrush.

Love,
Dr. Piggy

From: Mandel, Dr. Ellen
Sent: Wednesday, December 28, 2011, 4:48 p.m.
To: Maxam, Dr. Susan L.
Subject: Pre-China disaster

Perhaps the most outstanding pretrip disaster was two days before our trip to China on that "slow boat."

I feel that it is my genuine responsibility to have my hair coifed (and frizz proofed), of course, and a manicure and a pedicure.

Added to that was always large hair removal.

Were this not done, my husband and I could very well fight over his razor.

How lucky to have a mustache, furry brows, and I will cleverly stop there.

I went to the usual waxing person who waxed my brows, my lip, and my chin.

What makes even more of a treat is that a lot of this hair is white.

But alas, a new stunning me.

Ready for the trip that I still am not too thrilled with! Then off to Pace University to teach. I had time to sit in the sun for a half an hour for my pre-tan pretrip; I was thrilled!

No hair, and sunburn, ready for my movie contract!

During class, I started to feel a little strange.

My face was more blotchy than usual after waxing, and my upper lip was a teensy bit swollen.

It wasn't until I was approaching the bridge, not too far from home, that my face swelled up, and my throat started to close.

Holy shit, I was having an anaphylactic reaction.

The drama queen called her sister to say good-bye.

This was one way to get out of going to China, or anywhere else, for that matter.

I tried to speed toward Nyack Hospital, and my sister was smart enough to call ahead, so that the doctors were awaiting my arrival.

They pumped with Benadryl and prednisone and saved my life.

It seems that I had an allergic reaction to the waxing and sun combination, which of course no one had ever heard of before.

Always an overachiever.

In retrospect, having known that the trip to China was going to be so horrific, I would have asked them not to have done such a good job in reviving me.

Much, much love,
Dr. Piggy

From: Mandel, Dr. Ellen
Sent: Wednesday, December 28, 2011, 6:00 p.m.
To: Maxam, Dr. Susan L.
Subject: A slow boat to China

Dear Dr. Wiggy,

One of the most challenging (sucky, sucky, sucky) experiences of my life was my trip to China.

As I mentioned a couple of days ago, I had that terrible anaphylactic reaction to wax and sun.

The day and a half before we left, I was in Nyack Hospital, pumped with Benadryl and prednisone.

For most, a sizable dose of Benadryl puts one in a near-comatose state, but for us brain-injured it has the opposite effect.

Add to that sixty milligrams of Prednisone, and I became a raving lunatic.

(As if I am not nuts enough.)

This is not a face that needs to be red and swollen, nor one whose self-image to begin with is intact.

Therefore, I would have been very happy to sit in my house with—you know the old joke—two bags over my head, in case the first one fell off.

Surely a trip to China was not on my agenda for the next day, not then nor ever.

I had misgivings (terrors) about the trip long before the hospital thing.

This was a nineteen-day trip, a twenty-hour plane ride.

My husband tried to reassure me. I had a hunch, however, it wasn't going to be an ideal trip.

We were flying business class on an unmentioned airline. (I wouldn't want to be sued for slander.)

With three herniated discs and twenty hours, this in truth was the only way I could have flown.

It was a bad sign right off the start when it was early morning and the curtains were closed so as not to wake the passengers. Who sleeps at 9:00 a.m.?

Using the newest technology, the designers made the reclining seats of metal, and they looked just like coffins.

They were so high up and so peculiarly situated that all I could see of my husband was his arm, if he waved it in the air.

My husband, a much better adjusted person (as far as traveling is concerned) made himself comfortable.

Not so I.

I couldn't get the headphones on, I twisted the wires, the TV hit me in the head, and I couldn't put the seat in a comfortable position for my back.

All I could do was cry quietly.

Not so quietly, however—I got out of my seat to torture my husband on a semifrequent basis.

Finally in frustration, I took half a Xanax and slept for a whole three hours.

When I awoke, there were still several hours to go.

No, I did not want orange juice and eggs in the middle of the night, and no, I couldn't focus on reading when I was so agitated.

When we landed, it was very crowded in the airport.

We hurried to catch our next flight. That's right, two and a half hours to get from Hong Kong to Shanghai.

When we arrived in Shanghai, some hours on some morning, on some day (twelve-hour time difference), I was somewhat relieved.

But not for long.

The airline had lost our luggage.

And you know from my description of how I travel, I had everything that I owned in the world in those suitcases.

After one and a half hours, one of the two pieces of missing luggage was found.

Guess whose it wasn't.

How'd you guess?

I stood by the luggage retriever and cried and cried and cried some more.

Not long after my crying jag, my luggage was found.

When we exited the airport, the temperature was over one hundred degrees and the humidity 100 percent as well.

I was too delirious to care about anything actually—my life, David's life, any life.

I must admit that I was relieved to be out of the airport.

We were only a taxi ride away from our five-star hotel!

The driver, who weighed about as much as my thigh, spoke no English.

It was the drive of a lifetime.

The driver had been in one of those Jackie Chan movies, for sure.

He drove on winding roads at ninety miles an hour, throwing us from one side of the cab to another.

Hysterical crying was replaced by hysterical laughter.

We would die way before the trip was really under way.

When we arrived in the city, this guy couldn't find the hotel.

My husband managed to tell him the way.

About 10:00 p.m. we arrived at one of the most magnificent hotels I have ever seen.

We hadn't eaten, but soon thereafter we enjoyed delicious wonton soup.

Our room was gorgeous, and we slept.

Had we been able to spend more time in this luxurious hotel, it might have been a buffer for me.

The problem was, we were on a tour, and after an excellent breakfast, we left the hotel (7:30 a.m.) and didn't come back until midevening.

On that first morning, we met our thirty-eight tour mates (I already hated everybody; I was in that kind of mood) and our guide.

I have conveniently forgotten everyone's names—the whole thing was such a trauma—but I can picture each one of them.

They were really wonderful people.

Back to my tale of woe. The bus took us to a beautiful famous garden.

As we stepped off the bus, it was 107 degrees with once again 100 percent humidity.

I reminded myself that I didn't want to get off the plane when I got a whiff of Mexico's heat and humidity years ago, and how I would have given any amount of money to be able to complain in Mexico.

My face, still a drop swollen from the prednisone, was dripping wet, clothes wet, and hair frizzy ringlets plastered to my head.

This was a piece of cake (a favorite expression of mine) next to the sight of my husband.

My husband cannot tolerate the heat.

We keep our bedroom temperature at about sixty-six degrees.

He first bought an overcoat when he was past forty and wears shorts in December.

My husband looked as if he had just come out of the shower.

He looked like he was experiencing the beginning of a heat stroke.

He also has five stents.

We found, luckily, a Starbucks not far from this famous garden and stayed there until my husband felt better.

I was very upset when he didn't agree to permit me to spend the rest of the trip in Starbucks.

As an aside, I must tell you that there were millions of people everywhere and millions of cars.

As a result one is able to go nowhere fast. (I love that cliché.)

It was that day, or one day soon thereafter, that we were taken to the riverboat that was to be our home for six long days.

I love luxury, and this wasn't it. It was small, hot, and poorly ventilated, and it had mold growing in the shower, which leaked. My husband is the type who needs to be shown the second room first, so we changed our room three times.

We found out that everyone did. The rooms were all the same.

The first dinner was at a large round table.

As the waiter came around to take our orders, my eyes welled up with tears, and I ran out of the dining area and to my room.

When David arrived minutes thereafter, I could not be consoled.

This was as close to a panic attack as I had ever experienced.

I wanted to go home, and here we were in the middle of nowhere for six days.

I have suffered from depression and anxiety for years, but this was of another genre.

I couldn't keep it together.

There are no jokes here. I was humbled by the experience and have a deeper understanding and empathy for those who have these attacks.

My husband, whom I had made up my mind to kill after we got home, was really wonderful.

It also helped to speak to my daughter and sister to the tune of $409 in telephone charges.

I also stopped taking the prednisone, which I am sure had helped to put me over the edge.

The lunches and some dinners were usually eaten in local restaurants.

Local restaurants, local food.

Local food, and no eating for me.

We sat in groups of eight or ten. Dishes were served on lazy susans, which spun around fast.

One or two dishes were somewhat reasonable. (That's what David said, anyway. I was short and too slow to compete with flying forks.)

Several dishes were hot and spicy, and two dishes looked so bad that you could almost hear them woof.

My meals were all the same.

Eggs for breakfast at the hotel, veggies (bok choy, mostly) and a cup of rice for lunch, and the same for dinner.

Because I had embarrassed myself in front of the other passengers, I felt that I owed them an explanation.

You know the old saying "Quit while you're ahead"? Not me, not Dr. Blabbermouth here.

I told all about my meltdown—blah, blah, blah—and so they were nice but maybe a drop cautious.

They were a sturdy group, and they hardly complained.

I sure made up for them.

There was a ninety-two-year-old woman, wheelchair bound, who constantly had a smile on her face. This was so alien to me.

We were stuck in one of the rainstorms we had (it rained for fourteen out of sixteen days), and she kept smiling.

Finally, I had to approach her.

I told her that if she didn't stop smiling, I was going to smack her up and that she was ruining the trip for the rest of us.

I don't know how, but the six horrible days were over.

David said that I had some good times on the boat.

I told him that I was trying to make the best of it, and he laughed in my face.

We were now ready for the land portion of our trip (like I hadn't had enough).

We flew to five different cities. That's right, added fun!

Packing, repacking, packing, repacking.

Some flights two hours or a little less.

One or two days in one city and then on to the next.

Weather was the same in each—wet, hot, and humid!

All had beautiful hotels, which we were unable to spend much time in due to the rigorous touring schedule.

In one of the cities, we went by poorly air-conditioned bus to a famous zoo. We did see two adorable pandas, but most of the animals were smart enough to stay in their caves to avoid the heat.

We were the only dummies. In each city I looked uglier than in the city before. It was a cumulative effect. And that ninety-two-year-old bitch, fresh as a daisy, was still smiling.

The trip home was a blur. I was too euphoric knowing that we were going home.

I was also conjuring up ways to thank my David. Mama always said that you can't get arrested for thinking. When the plane landed and the doors opened, one grateful lady (me) touched American soil (the floor of the airport) and sang aloud the entire chorus of "God Bless America."

Love you,
Dr. Piggy

From: Mandel, Dr. Ellen
Sent: Sunday, March 18, 2012, 11:16 a.m.
To: Maxam, Dr. Susan L.
Subject: Who can you trust?

My dear Dr. Wiggy,

David is flying down to Atlanta in a few weeks to attend his half-brother's stepdaughter's bat mitzvah.

Remind me to tell you some time how he is an only child with seven brothers and sisters.

He had halves and steps long before it was so in.

Never realized how avant-garde he was.

And here I am married to the same man for almost forty-plus years!

Once again, a different world.

When thinking about Atlanta, it reminded me of a trip that we took to Atlanta, the four of us, eons ago, when the children were fairly young.

The three of them had more time off than I had, so I had made arrangements to fly home earlier.

The problem was that at the last minute, my flight was changed, and I had to notify my dad so that he could pick me up at a different airport.

The airport was packed, not a seat to be had, and I had to make my call.

What to do?

To make matters worse, my overpacked suitcase (back then, as now, following the take-everything-you-own plan) made it impossible to get to the phone.

Sitting down (how lucky they were) were two nice-looking gentlemen.

"Would you be kind enough to watch this suitcase for a minute?" I asked with a smile.

Sure, said the one sitting on the left.

I proceeded to the phone and made the new arrangements with my too-good-natured dad.

When I returned to the gentlemen, I extended my hand, only to find that when the gentleman extended his hand, he was handcuffed to the detective sitting next to him.

The man whom I had asked to help me was being extradited for some felony.

The men and many of the bystanders in the airport became hysterical laughing.

Shows to go you, I always had good judgment.

That's it for now, my dear friend,

Love,
Xxxxxooooo,
Dr. Piggy

From: Mandel, Dr. Ellen
Sent: Monday, August 5, 2013, 8:16 p.m.
To: Maxam, Dr. Susan L.
Subject: Watch out for terrorists

My divine Dr. Wiggy, VP (wonderful new title)

Of course the terrorist alert has been announced, right before David and I are going abroad.

I am not surprised!

Of course, I am very uncertain as to what one does when one gets this good news.

I am glad that it no way implies that I should pack less!

I am of course willing and able to abort the trip, being the gifted traveler that I am.

I was willing to cancel before the alert.

But you know David!

He has been planning this trip since last year, and terrorists or not, here we come!

We are flying to London, taxiing to Southampton, and meeting our cruise ship, the *Celebrity Eclipse.*

We will be seeing parts of Europe that we have already seen, and adding to the list—Bruges in Belgium and Berlin in Germany.

Since our last cruise, that Italian ocean liner that capsized and the Carnival poopie ship have come and gone, and this has made a terrific impression on me.

Add to the mix terrorists and the like, and would you or anyone in his or her right mind want to go?

You know years ago, the only terrorist I worried about was my mother with her powerful left arm.

And today, it is, I am afraid, a totally different story.

Aside from canceling one's flight, there is really no protocol to follow that I am aware of.

Of course, now I won't sit next to anyone at the airport, because who knows who they really are.

I am often suspicious of people without an alert (I think there are places for people like me called asylums).

If people smile at me, I will suspect them; if they don't smile at me, I will suspect them; and if they have a blank stare, I will really suspect them.

Notice how it always comes back to me (a true narcissist).

I didn't know what I was going to do during the seven-hour flight, and now I will be busy, suspecting everybody and worrying.

I am hoping that the five milligrams of Xanax will put me out of my misery.

Love u,
Dr. Piggy

From: Mandel, Dr. Ellen
Sent: Sunday, December 29, 2013, 1:13 p.m.
To: Maxam, Dr. Susan L.
Subject: More traveling, more fears

My dearest Dr. VP and hopefully Assoc. Provost Wiggy,

Hopefully by now, you are in the Caribbean with your delightful family in the lap of luxury.

This dysfunctional traveler is revving up for her next adventure.

Hope it won't be like the cruise we heard about last week.

You remember, for more than three days, the passengers had doo-doo and sewage in the halls and rooms with a stench in every cabin.

It wouldn't have taken me three days to jump overboard as a pleasant alternative.

This time around, it is the ship stuck in ice around the Antarctic that I'm fixated on. I noticed that no one has been rescued yet, because none of the rescue ships that have been sent have the equipment needed to cut through the ice.

Yesterday on the news I heard that the passengers were still happy.

They must have served them laughing water. (Does that really exist?) There wouldn't be enough Xanax in the world to keep me from delirium.

They said there was plenty of food for the passengers to eat.

That's what many of these passengers need! When the ice thaws in April and the passengers return, there will be a first-come, first-served for the gastric bypass procedure.

The procedure for the couple of days before we meet the ship appears to be foolproof!

Tuesday morning I am going to David's office with David. He will see patients, and when he is finished, we will proceed to the Newark Marriott at the airport so we can make our early flight Wednesday morning to Miami.

As soon as I mentioned that I would wander around Englewood while he therapized, he went a little nuts and vetoed my plan.

The last time I did this wandering, I tripped over my own foot, fell down hard, broke my nose, and was taken by ambulance, full of blood, to Englewood Hospital.

I fell only about a hundred feet (said one hundred because I wanted you to think I knew my stuff, could have been a thousand feet for all I know).

Anyway, as the ambulance door was closed, and David yelled in, "Are we definitely not going?" I gave him some look and then off to the hospital!

Love you,
Dr. Piggy

CHAPTER 6

My Favorite Obsessions: Hair and Weight

From: Mandel, Dr. Ellen
Sent: Wednesday, December 6, 2011, 6:39 p.m.
To: Maxam, Dr. Susan L.
Subject: Who cares about hair anyway? Everyone!

Dear Dr. Wiggy,

I was looking at myself in the mirror early this morning, watching my hair grow.

Problem—haircut too short.

Other times hair left too long.

I remembered Jackie Mason's line about the Jewish holidays being either early or late each year, but never on time.

Is it not the same, I thought, with haircuts—too short or too long but never just right.

Hair is a repetitive theme in my life.

I was born with a full head of wavy black hair.

Those who knew my father claimed that I looked like "dad in a blankie."

With all due respect, that wasn't a good thing!

As me and my hair grew, I turned into a pretty little girl.

So pretty that I modeled for Harry Conover, one of the top children's modeling agencies.

This modeling career was celebrated briefly, although I am not exactly sure when my looks went south.

The next thing I remember, I was going to the beauty parlor (no such thing as a salon) fairly regularly with mom.

Most little girls would love this.

But then, they were not afraid of the waxer who showed up regularly at the salon to wax the floor.

Let me define waxer, since it is used in a different context today, as the man hired by the beauty parlor to wax the floors and shop and make them shine.

By ages ten or eleven, ponytails were in, so the wavy and now fully developed, frizzy black hair was under control.

I wore my hair in a ponytail.

For several years, I thought that I was Asian, due to the fact that my mother pulled my hair so tight that my eyes slanted.

In the front, I wore bangs, cut on a slant, so I looked like Hitler.

As if this coif weren't scary enough, it was the style to have flowers and other accessories flying around the ponytail or chopsticks that dug into my head.

As a teenager, the summers were brutal.

Large orange-juice cans were used before rollers to straighten one's frizzy locks.

Straightenings were becoming the must for frizzy hair.

Unless one could afford the pricey straightening, one settled on the cheaper version.

Those who in desperation tried the latter came out as though they had been run over by a lawn mower.

Sister Sooz's Hair Stories

With all due respect to my sister's stories of woe about her hair, my hair makes hers look like silk. My hair is so awful that it makes Kramer's hair from *Seinfeld* look sleek. My hair is so awful that if I let it dry without blowing it, no one gives me eye contact. My hair is so awful that there aren't enough hats to cover it at the beach or on a misty day. My hair doesn't even dry south of Virginia, and it has been the cause of much grief and attention throughout my time.

As a little girl, I would boast, "I have naturally curly hair," with the emphasis on "naturally." Little did I know that it would be the bane of my existence.

During the summer of my fifteenth year, my parents were able to send me to sleepaway camp, something I had always wanted to do. The summer was great, but unfortunately, as my hormones kicked in that summer, so did the kink in my hair. By the time my parents came up for visiting day, on a hot, humid day, my hair had taken on a life of its own. I was overdue for a haircut and although I was only five-two, my hair made me look like five-five. My mother didn't want to make me feel self-conscious, but I could see her eyes lifting up to the top of my head as if she did not know where it would end. (BTW, I did have a boyfriend that year, and either I must have had some other charming qualities or he was visually impaired.) Anyway, there were no cell phones in those days, or my mother would have scheduled an emergency straightening on their ride home to Brooklyn. I think I went directly from the camp bus to the beauty parlor, and from the age of fifteen until the present, hair straightening has made my life much easier. (As if that's all it takes to make life easy!) I am sixty-six years old and still looking in every mirror as I pass, hoping against hope that my hair has turned straight. That hasn't happened yet.

Here are some of the hair stories that followed…

One that sticks in my mind the most took place almost forty-five years ago, when my husband, Marty, and I, at the ages of twenty-two and twenty-one, took our wedding gift money and planned a six-week trip to Europe on five dollars a day (a la Arthur Frommer). Actually, it was probably ten dollars a day, which kept us out of student hostels and insane asylums, most of the time.

In preparation for our trip, the discussion of taking or leaving my hair dryer came up. Women did not blow their hair dry in those days. We had big plastic hooded hair dryers that we sat under after we washed and set our hair in rollers. We did not wash our hair every day, but we set it every night. The equipment involved was rollers, clips, and hairnets. (This was not attractive, but we all did it.) Marty realized that taking the hair dryer would be another thing to schlep and the number of suitcases (or valises, as we called them then) was getting rather big. I wanted to take the hair dryer, and Marty did not want to take it. We presented our case to my mother-in-law, a quiet, wonderful lady whom I got to know for just a while before she died of pancreatic cancer. We each stated our cases, and Marty's mom said we should do an experiment. She told me to wash my hair and not blow it dry, and then we would evaluate the situation. I hopped in the shower and washed my hair and did not blow it dry. When I returned, my mother-in-law took one look at me and in an instant said, "Take the hair dryer."

I hated to do something that Marty did not want to do, so I came up with a solution. In the past, I had had my hair straightened at Kenneth's beauty salon in the city, and it made it much more manageable. I would get my hair straightened, and that would solve the problem. It turned out that Kenneth's was very costly, and so I settled for one of the cheaper, more factory-like establishments. I had it straightened, and though it did not look as nice and smooth as when Kenneth's did it, I was satisfied that this was the answer to my problem.

Off to Europe we went, and my hair behaved most of the time. Life was good. Toward the end of our trip, we stopped in a city called Zaragoda, a few hours from Madrid, where we would be staying for a few days. The inn we stayed in was rather quaint (a euphemism for pretty old and not expensive) and actually had its own pool. I was going to wash my hair the night that we arrived in Zaragoda, and so in a free-spirited way, I jumped into the pool and swam without a bathing cap (another must in the seventies in the States). We went up to our room and I showered before dinner. I put a small amount of shampoo on my hair, and I immediately noticed a problem. My hair turned to glue. I didn't know what was happening, and so I called upon Marty for his help. He got in the shower with me, and I instructed him to use the conditioner. As he tried to rinse my hair, bubbles began to form. They wouldn't stop. I looked like a human chemistry experiment. It seems that the chlorine in the water and the chemicals in my hair had mixed and were creating a very bad situation. He tried to comb it through, but broke a few combs in the process. By this time, I was hysterically crying, and we finally gave up, and I came out of the shower and got dressed for the evening. There was nothing I could do with my hair. I finally put it in a perpendicular ponytail and upon looking in the mirror, declared that I was not going to dinner. After some coercing, we went to dinner, and I cried through most of the meal. I didn't know what I was going to do. We knew that our first stop in Madrid, instead of the renowned Prado Museum, would be a beauty parlor. Of course, being in Spain, everyone in the shop spoke Spanish, and via a scary game of charades, they indicated that they thought it best that they cut most of my hair off. I was now more hysterical, but luckily, I remembered my French and found someone who spoke that language. We decided to try a neutralizing conditioner that would undo the effects of the chemical problem. In fact, my hair returned to a normal-enough state, and we were able to go about the rest of our trip without incidents. My hair remained a bit wiry and broken, but at least it was still on my head.

Next hair story…

The gut-wrenching realization that my naturally curly hair was less than a gift from God took place as soon as we relocated to the Twin Cities in Minnesota, where my husband, Marty, would be in a doctoral program for three years, and I would take my master's and teach math.

I truly expected that moving from the Northeast to the Midwest would naturally be a culture shock. What I didn't expect was 'hair shock'. A majority of Minnesotans had silky blond hair and few had ever seen a head of hair like mine! I was to find this out as soon as I went to a beauty salon to have my hair "done".

I decided to try out a not-very-expensive place to have my hair "done." As I mentioned, there were no hair blowers in those days. Our hair was "set" in rollers, and we stayed under hair dryers in the beauty salon. I was looking forward to relaxing and letting someone else deal with my hair when things took a turn for the worse. The hairstylist began getting her tools ready, among which were very tiny rollers. "I wouldn't do that if I were you," I said. "My hair needs big, humungous rollers resembling orange juice cans."

"Sorry, we don't have anything bigger." What could I do but give the go-ahead? To make matters worse, as other groups of women came and went from under the drier, as their hair dried, mine would not dry. The salon workers kept checking my hair to see if it was dry. Surely, this woman's head must be dry. Finally, after one and a half hours, feeling very hot and looking beet red, I was cooked. The next step was to comb out my hair that had been in teeny rollers for all this time. Suffice to say that by the time the beautician was finished, she told me not to tip her. Not only did I tip her, I thanked her and proceeded to run out to where Marty met a hysterically crying woman.

I am not a mature woman, mother, and grandmother, and so I try to put things in perspective. It didn't help when my oldest grandson said that I looked like a sheep, and the second one at a similar age, on a humid day, said, "Nan, what did you do to your hair? Do you want to borrow my hat?"

My friends still think that I exaggerate. If I had the nerve, I would let them see a picture with my "natural" curl, but I am too vain! I have made my daughter-in-law, Dina, who also has "naturally curly" hair, promise to straighten my hair (or at least the bangs) if I become incapable of doing it myself, or, worse yet, I deny that there is a problem.

Do you think that it's odd that when I was told I had to be hospitalized for serious ailments, my first computation was how many days to my hair dye and keratin treatment?

Love you and love Sooz,
Dr. Piggy

From: Mandel, Dr. Ellen
Sent: Friday, December 7, 2012, 2:58 p.m.
To: Maxam, Dr. Susan L.
Subject: How to become bulimic without even trying

Dear Dr. Wiggy,

Had a few minutes to think about my weight, with the holiday season upon us. I really don't obsess about it much; I keep it down in general to about seventeen hours a day.

It is not difficult to trace the problem back to my roots.

I probably had the only Jewish mother, in Jewish-mother history, who grabbed the food I ate right out of my mouth.

My mother had been a size forty-two dress and weighed over two hundred pounds until she was sixteen years old.

After that, she miraculously lost a hundred pounds on the "Pep and milk diet" (I think that Pep was the modern-day cornflakes, or Cheerios, or something like that).

In an effort to protect me from becoming fat, she enabled me to have many food issues. Her actions and her attitude, though well intended, did much damage.

Within the many years of my continuous struggle with my weight were some very funny situations, which I will share. My Pop-Pop would introduce my sister and me to customers in the store (my grandparents owned a ladies' lingerie and children's clothing store) with the phrase, "This is the smart one [my sister], and this is the one with a tendency to be stout." What made a bad situation worse was that my sister weighed thirty-six pounds at six years of age and could eat whatever she wanted.

My mother always let me taste whatever she ordered.

Much to my dismay, she loved cottage cheese, grapefruit, and other disgustingly healthy foods.

She was lucky that I didn't kill her when I heard her ordering.

When I was about age four, before my sister was old enough to order anything, my mother bought six éclairs from Ebinger's Bakery for dinner one Friday night.

I discovered them in the refrigerator, at about 3:00 p.m.

I begged her to let me have one, but it was out of the question.

The three-hour wait was simply too long.

When no one was looking, I went down to the store (we lived upstairs) and took a straight pin from my nanny's work table.

I quickly removed the éclairs in question, made a hole in each one big enough to suck the custard out with my straw.

I might have been safe, were it not for my Pop-Pop, who announced, "They are just not making these éclairs the way they used to."

I remember being removed from the table by my ear.

To this day, I think it was worth it!

Weight issues during my pregnancies also led to some funny situations.

In my day, a pregnant woman was permitted to gain up to twenty-five pounds before her ob gyn admonished her.

For my monthly visit, I removed my clothes—in the examining room, that is—but also I noticed the other women all sitting in the very hot waiting room with no air-conditioning (which coincidentally was always going to be fixed, only not in my lifetime) were hardly showing. I was in maternity clothes in my second month, and although I gained only twenty-five pounds with my son, by the eighth month, I looked like I would deliver my son along with his carriage.

I was to deliver by C-section, but my water broke before the scheduled day. It was much less comfortable than it is today, I am told, but between my gorgeous new baby boy and the prospect of losing weight after his birth, I was ecstatic. The second day postop, it was very difficult to get out of bed, but the scale was only a hallway away.

I forced myself to stand up, moaned my way down the hallway, and voila, "Mecca." One didn't have to be a rocket scientist to figure out that with the baby weighing a hair under seven pounds, and water weight, and so forth, there should be a significant loss. With glee, I took the lightest step, with one foot, and so carefully added the second foot, and then, I started to scream.

The nurses and doctors came to my aid from all direction, expecting to find me prone on the floor in a pool of blood.

They found, rather, a woman who, in disbelief, had lost only two pounds.

Disappointed and embarrassed, I schlepped my fat back to my room.

An hour or so thereafter, I overheard a woman in the next room asking her husband to bring her old jeans, then called dungarees.

I asked my husband to bring half a valium and an old tent.

Love,
Dr. Piggy

From: Mandel, Dr. Ellen Saturday,
Sent: December 7, 2013, 3:57 p.m.
To: Maxam, Dr. Susan L.
Subject: Not meant to run

My dearest Dr. Vice President Wiggy,

Unable to shut my mouth and lose some weight and tired of asking the salesgirl in Lord and Taylor for the size tremendous department, I decided that perhaps a little exercise would help me at least lose some inches, if not weight.

Because many of my good intentions have remained just that—good intentions—I did not invest in a "walking wardrobe."

Having so many wardrobes already, in my large closet in the basement (the are-you-kidding wardrobe, pleasingly plump wardrobe, and the you-might-as-well-stay-home-in-bed wardrobe), I decided to make do with what I had.

I began walking at home initially to test the waters.

This went well enough, except for the black and blues, gotten from bump ing into major pieces of furniture along my limited route.

I decided to venture outside and walk partway around Rockland Lake.

I was no stranger to Rockland Lake, having walked around with my husband, although never consistently, and never at a really good pace.

Mine was more strolling, and not totally without incidents.

One spring, while looking at the heron that my husband pointed out, I missed a step and sprained my ankle.

This time would be different.

This was serious business!

I set out by myself and couldn't help noticing these "professional athletes."

The women were tall (there must be some short women in Rockland) and built like racehorses, long and lean (the worst kind).

They wore running suits in black with vivid colors, trimming and rimming, headbands to keep their hair (straight, I might add) out of their eyes, fashionable sneakers, and insulated gloves.

I was also fashionable with my will-make-do outfit: gray sweats and no accessories.

Au natural!

Five minutes after I began walking and a little jogging thrown in, my hair, which needed to be cut yesterday, started to frizz and seemed to take on a life of its own.

After ten minutes I started to shvitz (sweat big time).

This flattened the frizz to create one of the most unbelievable coiffures known to man.

The elastic in my gray sweats was not adequate, so I was forced to hold up the pants at both thighs, so as not to lose them.

Thank God I didn't meet anyone I knew.

The "professional athletes" glided by, intact (no sweating, not a hair out of place, and they were not holding on to their pants).

I finally arrived at my car. Hallelujah!

I will be going to bump into my furniture in my house real soon.

In fact, I can't wait.

It has become even more obvious to me that some people just can't make do and shouldn't try.

Well, my favorite lady, let me know how you like this,

Xxooo,
Dr. Piggy

From: Mandel, Dr. Ellen
Sent: Friday, July 4, 2014, 8:44 a.m.
To: Maxam, Dr. Susan L.
Subject: The nasty dogs in Cannes

Good morning, Dr. Wiggy,

At least my hair didn't turn green. One time (that's right) it really did turn green.

Lost my mind?

No referring to my hair after my Keratin hair-straightening process on Tuesday.

Since they removed the formaldehyde, it is a safer process.

And if there is a little formaldehyde in it, so I croak a month earlier. Must be something bad in it, because the hairdresser and the shampoo lady wear masks.

Also, now that I think of it, I was moved to an isolated spot of the shop, and I was told to close my eyes through most of the process.

It reminds me of when David and I were in Cannes in 1970, a place where I ate my own weight in Grand Marnier crepes.

We stayed at the best hotels in the world but saved money by traveling on the Eurail pass.

By the time we arrived at this snooty hotel, it was our last stop, and I looked like it was my last stop.

Hair, unimaginable, drew crowds, and so forth.

When we checked in, I asked for an appointment at their beauty salon.

No joke, I was sent back to the back room, where all the French poodles and other assorted dogs with their noses in the hair were being coiffed.

They didn't talk to me, and I wouldn't speak to them either.

But when they barked, I knew what they were discussing!

Matthew and "Wild Jake" are coming for the annual Fourth of July barbeque, and unless there is lightning and thunder, the show must go on.

This will hopefully be followed by the Macy's fireworks displays along the East River.

As children, we went to Coney Island to watch this wonderful phenomenon,

Everyone loved it except me, who stayed in the hot car, too afraid of the fireworks (always well adjusted). In those pioneer days, you could stay in the car without worrying about being kidnapped. Also remember what I told you my father said: "Whoever can lift you can have you."

Nothing left to one's imagination as to why my eating disorder was always alive and well.

Well that's it for now, my sweetie pie.

Really need to get hold of that list for the Komen Race.

Get back to me soon.

"And the land of the free, and the home of the brave."

Xxxoooo,
Dr. Piggy

CHAPTER 7

HOLIDAYS

From: Mandel, Dr. Ellen
Sent: November 27, 2012, 8:20 p.m.
To: Maxam, Dr. Susan L.
Subject: Thanksgiving has gone to the dogs

Years ago, Thanksgiving was one of the most treasured holidays of the year. Family would gather from near and far to eat a delicious feast, which was traditionally prepared by the mama. A million traditional side dishes accompanied Tom Turkey, and every family member was as stuffed as the turkey they ate. There was turkey, stuffing, cranberry sauce, candied yams, and a large garden variety of fresh pies. They all left the table having consumed their own weight in food.

When our Leigh came in from college, there was always the question as to who would take Leigh to the airport to return to the University of Wisconsin. I wonder if hearing "I took him last time" or "it's not my turn" was responsible for his going into therapy for a while after graduation. Nah!

Today, Thanksgiving is still celebrated, but it seems to be a little different. I didn't realize quite how much this treasured day has changed until I heard about my friend's Thanksgiving extravaganza.

Thanksgiving is one of the few holidays that my friend doesn't spend with her birth family.

Rather, she goes to her friend's house.

Her friend's family is brilliant, successful, and quiet. I had never known quiet until I met her friend's family.

They were twenty-five diverse people. There were five vegetarians, six children, two dogs, and a cat. Two of the grownups were diabetic. One of the diabetics was also a vegetarian, while another woman who was a vegetarian also had colitis and couldn't eat dairy. This would have been quite enough for one Thanksgiving meal were it not for the fact that there were three pets also in attendance. It was not known if the pets were diabetic, but the jury was out as to whether they would have been vegetarians had they been asked their preference. Dog number one was a gorgeous, playful, large jumping dog, which belonged to the people whose house the dinner was in.

Dog number two was an old dog, a nonjumper, but somewhat of a glutton when food was around. Number three pet was a neurotic cat who must stay on a leash at all times. He must have a really fine disposition. He doesn't care for people, and I am very sure that most people aren't crazy about him. Neurotic me would be worried for the whole night whether he would break away from his leash and claw everyone at the table.

I wish I had been a fly on the wall to see the dishes that were made to accommodate the variety of tastes and illnesses. I'd sure like to cook for the diabetic vegetarian with colitis.

Xxxoo,
Dr. Piggy

From: Mandel, Dr. Ellen
Sent: Friday, December 14, 2012, 3:24 p.m.
To: Maxam, Dr. Susan L.
Subject: The Eight Days of Chanukah

MY DEAR Dr. Wiggy,

Just CHECKING UP ON YOU AND I MIGHT ADD THAT I HAVE NO CLUE HOW TO GET RID OF THE CAPS OR HOW THEY CAME ON MY SCREEN ANYWAY.

I AM PLANNING TO FIGURE IT OUT IN MY NEXT LIFE, WHERE I WILL ALSO BE TALL, BLOND, AND THIN.

THANK GOD TOMORROW IS THE LAST DAY OF CHANUKAH.

I HATE TO CRITICIZE GOD, BUT IT SURE WASN'T NICE OF HIM TO MAKE IT EIGHT DAYS.

THE HECK WITH THE OIL.

THE NEW TREND AMONG JEWS IS TO PROVIDE THEIR LITTLE DEARS WITH ONE GIFT FOR EACH NIGHT, EIGHT GIFTS IN ALL.

MY SISTER AND I WERE WELL TAKEN CARE OF, BUT RECEIVED FOUR OR SO GIFTS WITH TWO BEING CLOTHES, WHICH NEVER COUNTED.

WHAT KID NEEDS EIGHT GIFTS?

AND TODAY THEY ARE BIG-TICKET ITEMS.

NINE- AND TEN-YEAR-OLDS ARE RECEIVING IPHONES.

SOME PARENTS TOLD ME THAT IT WAS FOR SAFETY REASONS. IT IS FOR SAFETY FOR THEIR KIDS, OR THEY DON'T HAVE TO INTERACT WITH THEIR LITTLE TOOTSIES, WHO ARE ON THE PHONE ALL DAY.

CYNICAL? JUST A TAD!

Oh wow, where did that caps lock come from?

Glad I noticed it right away, huh?

Well, my dear friend, have to enter my grades.
Once again, let me know how you are doing.
I would like to help you through the holidays if I can in any way.

Love you,
Dr. Piggy

From: Mandel, Dr. Ellen
Sent: November 30, 2013, 10:00 a.m.
To: Maxam, Dr. Susan L.
Subject: Celebrating Chanukah on Thanksgiving (or the Pilgrims and the Macabees)

Dear Dr. Wiggy,

Let me say just a few words about celebrating Chanukah on Thanksgiving.

It sucks!

It is very good for the confused population, don't you think?

As if we don't consume enough calories when Thanksgiving stands by itself.

I had my menorah on the table with little turkeys flying around.

Turkeys and latkes, pumpkin pie, and jelly donuts.

Carving the turkey after lighting the menorah.

We gather together to ask the Lord's blessing followed by Chanukah, oh Chanukah.

Good news.

I won't be here in the seventy or so thousand years when this happens again.

And God forbid I am still here. I'll kill myself.

Xxxxxxooooo,
Dr. Piggy

From: Mandel, Dr. Ellen
Sent: Friday, June 27, 2014, 10:12 p.m.
To: Maxam, Dr. Susan L.
Subject: A wonderful Father's Day

The Father's Day celebration (birthday celebration) turned out to be a wonderful one. Twenty-two people were in attendance. It is always a challenge foodwise, because my son-in-law's parents are Hassidic Jews and have to be provided with special glatt kosher food. The paper plates are never a problem because Susannah uses only paper plates. My mother probably turns over in her grave over the plates and cutlery.

I, the Jewish mother/mother-in-law, remain silent, and no longer suggest, recommend, and so forth.

Marie Antoinette said, "Let them eat cake," but she never mentioned paper or china, so I guess it is not important.

Sometimes there is a fight inside me—tradition or not so important.

I guess each person has to draw his or her own line.

Four of the guests, whom I have met several times before, were absolutely captivating.

Sam's grandma Selma, a recent widow, always invites her three dearest friends to celebrate with us.

Selma and Estelle and her husband are all in their late eighties, while Bernice (also a widow) is ninety-two. She still drives her ninety-five-year-old girlfriend to the supermarket.

The little group, who have been friends for decades, who raised their families together in Levittown, Long Island, define growing old gracefully. Grandma Selma is a sculptress, Grandma Estelle ran a bakery for many years, and Grandma Bernice belongs to many organizations. They are riddled with physical problems (two walk with canes, one frequently uses a walker). They are sharp as tacks and have strong opinions. They are interested and interesting. (I wonder if they mind paper plates.)

They don't complain, and health is never placed on their conversation agenda.

What's wrong with these people that they don't complain? They remind me of that nice little ninety-two-year-old lady traveling with her wheelchair in China in some famous square who smiled even though it rained on all of us for three hours. She was the one who I was forced to tell that if she didn't stop smiling, I would be forced to push her wheelchair down the hill.

Sometimes one is forced to take matters into one's own hands, now isn't one?

Bernice was showcased last year (2013) in a book entitled *The Privilege of Aging: Portraits of Twelve Jewish Women,* written by Patricia Gottlieb Shapiro.

What these twelve women have in common is their age (75–102), their vitality in handling their aging, and their person at the end of the day everyone bidding each other fond farewell.

A beautiful Father's Day/birthday was enjoyed by all.

Before Selma returned to Florida (where else?), she gave me the book *The Privilege of Aging,* and I read it voraciously.

It has given me a new perspective on my own life, and perhaps it can inspire all of us—young, old, very old. The author points out that the resources for successful aging are within all of us. We need to meet the challenges on creativity and growth that enable all of us to age without fear. I am starting to complain just an itsy-bitsy drop less.

I should admit to you before closing that I am still afraid of dying.

"What is it about dying that you are afraid of?" my sister asked me yesterday.

"I don't like change," I replied.

Good night, Dr. Wiggy.
Dr. Piggy

CHAPTER 8

In Sickness and in Health

From: Mandel, Dr. Ellen
Sent: Friday, February 17, 2012, 7:55 p.m.
To: Maxim, Dr. Susan L.
Subject: To stent or not to stent

Good evening, Dr. Wiggy, my friend,

Another so-not-boring day.

David had an angiogram this morning.

The pneumonia prevented me from accompanying him to our condo in Mt. Sinai.

Susannah came to the rescue and picked David up at 6:00 a.m. for the trek.

At Thirty-Fifth and Fifth, the car lost its steering, and David was headed for a wall.

Don't know how he avoided it and proceeded to Ninety-Ninth Street and Madison, where he found a good spot.

Susannah accompanied David to the check-in, where both of them called the AAA.

Susannah left David waiting and met the AAA person at the car.

The car was towed to Fifty-Seventh and somewhere, where it remained all day, having its alternator and belts changed to the tune of nine hundred dollars.

When Susannah returned to the hospital, David was right where she had left him.

They were running late.

What else is new?

To make a short story long, the procedure took more than twice the time it usually takes so that my stress level at home was pretty high.

David had scar tissue in the artery, which had to be removed. No stent!

Thank God for a job well done!

They gave him a large dose of valium before and after the surgery.

My son, Leigh, suggested that it was a good time while he was gaga from the drugs to tell him about the price of the car.

Everybody has his number.

What was refreshing was that Susannah, who had learned from the best mentor (that would be me), waited for David to be taken up and then hit the street.

She walked along Madison Avenue and bought a ring, bracelet, and necklace.

Not bad work in an hour and a half.

Nobody was surprised since everyone knew that during all the trillion times I have been to Mt. Sinai, my first stop is coffee and second the gift shop.

There should be at least one iota of joy in an otherwise horrible day.

Much love,
Dr. Piggy

From: Mandel, Dr. Ellen
Sent: Thursday, March 28, 2013
To: Maxam, Dr. Susan L.
Subject: It wasn't my time yet.

My dearest Dr. Wiggy,

It was the night before Christmas—nah.

How about it was the best of times, it was the worst of times—nah.

There was nothing dramatic about Thursday morning, March 21, 2013.

I was at my friend Anna's bakery having my morning coffee.

Since I didn't have to teach at Pace that morning, I had the brilliant idea of going into town to buy some jellybeans.

Doesn't every sane person crave jelly beans at eight fifteen in the morning?

Oddly enough, I was minding my own business, waiting to pick out all the orange beans, when this insane woman in a large SUV hit my Altima on the driver's side with such impact that my car became airborne, jumped the divide, went into the wooded area, and hit a tree,

I don't remember much, but I knew that I was hurt. I couldn't move my neck.

Being the drama queen that I am, I've always wanted to stop traffic, but this wasn't quite what I had in mind.

The police, paramedics, fire department, and my own fabulous family were wonderful.

They took me to the hospital that is known for its great emergency care.

If you have to get admitted, there is a fifty-fifty chance that you will live to get out, but you can't win them all.

The team was professional and thorough.

I was CAT scanned up the kazoo, and although there were no fractures, there were plenty of other neck injuries.

This will be a long recovery.

God had me in the palm of his hand.

It is amazing to me to be able to fit in the palm of anyone's hand.

God thought out loud, "She isn't a spring chicken. On the other hand, there is no worse complainer in the world," he continued. "I'm patient, but who would stand that woman twenty-four-seven? Nope, I'm sending her back for a while longer."

And so he did!

Xxxooo,
Dr. Piggy

From: Mandel, Dr. Ellen
Sent: Friday, March 29, 2013, 6:55 p.m.
To: Maxam, Dr. Susan L.
Subject: Checkout time in the ER

My dearest Dr. Wiggy,

Checkout time at the emergency room is greatly dissimilar from hotel checkout time.

At your luxury hotel out by noon.

After the tests have been taken and the doctor has examined you once, it could be days until you are seen again.

If they are busy, then the discharge papers could take months.

The tests were quick, and I thought that I overheard the CAT scan nurse say no neck fracture.

I was brought down from the CAT test and returned to my trendy cubicle.

When will I be given the results? I inquired.

What will happen, I was told, will be that the results will be sent to the ER, and when the ER doctor has time (and that is the key word around here, "time"), he will come in with your results. Then the discharge nurse, when she has time (another key word), will take out your IV and have you sign the discharge papers.

Let's see, I thought to myself, I will be out for my sixty-seventh birthday on May 8.

My sister, Sooz, who is one of the treasures in this world, looked at my face and knew that there wasn't a shot in hell that I was staying much longer.

I kept annoying the nurse who was in view to find out when the CAT scan results were coming down. After several sweet, sweet, sweet but annoying inquiries, she hurried up the process, and they arrived. The next nurse who saw me called the doctor, because I had removed my own neck brace.

This was so alien to my sister.

He had the miraculous test results with him.

No fracture, but plenty of injury to my poor old neck.

I told him that I would have no problem taking out my own IV.

I was discharged ten minutes thereafter.

Love,
Dr. Piggy

From: Mandel, Dr. Ellen
Sent: April 4, 2013
To: Maxam, Dr. Susan L.
Subject: Susannah's nose and why I wanted to break it.

My dear Dr. Wiggy,

Thrilled to see you!

You look fabulous.

So glad to be rid of the heavy neck brace (Hurrah!). Now I have a lighter one.

Therapy a long process for sure.

Let me continue with my sad tale!

I must digress a bit before to the ER.

I am in a heavy neck apparatus about as comfortable as a sharp stick in the eye.

Good news finally comes from the ER physician—no fracture.

Susannah, at the foot of the bed, shouts out, "Mom, now you can take care of me all next week when I have my nose job."

"That's exactly what came to my mind," I replied, even before wondering when I will have any motion of my neck to the right, even before wondering what meds I will need for this pain, or when will I be able to work again. "How about letting me get up from the f–– bed first?" I added.

She later apologized for thinking only of herself, and of course I forgave her, but I still haven't quite forgiven myself.

Maybe our generation gave too much to our kids.

I must not leave this as my final portrait of my beautiful, kind, caring, wonderful daughter.

Maybe I spoiled her just a tad!

My mother, God rest her soul, used to tell me that life can change in a split second, and it did.

A few days later, neck brace and all, my son-in-law drove me and Susannah to this magnificent office on Park Avenue for her new nosedo.

On our arrival at the reception desk, nurse inquired which one of us was the patient.

Damned if I knew.

Susannah hugged me and went in to the surgical procedural room.

We were told that we would be spending most of the afternoon there.

My son-in-law is addicted to whatever the hell games are played on his phone, iPad, and so forth.

He was in some sort of trance, playing on his iPad, iPhone, and so forth. At one point he took what he later called a power nap.

I took a power nothing.

I was worried about my child in the operating room.

Was everything going well? Would she be happy with her new nose, even though there was nothing wrong with her old nose?

How much discomfort would she be in?

For both of our sakes, I prayed for easy sailing.

How ridiculous of me (easy sailing).

I paced back and forth, took my pain meds, and gave out deep sighs (always a diva), and then I started to notice that the other doctor, an Italian gentleman who looked like an opera singer rather than a surgeon, was seeing patient after patient.

As he glided into the waiting room, very taken with himself, he greeted each woman with pretty much the same line: "You look fabulous, simply magnificent, a goddess."

"Holy shit," I said to myself. "Are we looking at the same people?" I saw women even older than I with faces pulled pretty tight, with faces that could stop a clock or make it run, as my aunt Cele would say.

Not all mind you, but enough to wonder what did these beauties look like before they had their work done?

Thank God Susannah had the other doctor.

More pacing, more waiting, more worrying.

Several visits to the lavatory, bathroom too commonplace for this office, and I was taken by the magnificent furnishings besides the toilet.

Gorgeous walls, pictures, mirrors, vanities.

Nah, it wouldn't look nice if I stole that gorgeous potted plant right out of there.

And my son-in-law, God bless his soul, still on that iPhone, iPad, or whatever.

After about an hour and a half, Miss Smiley nurse comes out to tell us that Susannah is doing fine.

This report is one of the perks that goes along with the $13,000 package.

I tell her that I am more interested in how the doctor is doing.

I now have no trouble filling the remaining time.

From nerves I visit the lavatory every twenty minutes (still dreaming up new maneuvers to steal the potted plant).

I pace and pace, watch more fairly ugly-looking "goddesses" coming out of the other doctor's office (easily collections are over a million for the day), and continue watching my son-in-law, in utter amazement, as he plays with his iPhone, iPad, and so forth.

After one more hour, the nurse reappears. "Princess Petunia" is out of the operating room and is in recovery.

When I ask how long she will be in recovery for, the nurse tells me that it varies from patient to patient. No one in our group ever really recovers from whatever they have, and in my family, we take the average time and multiply it by at least three.

Sure enough she takes longer than most.

Now she wants to see her husband and me, and we are ready for the viewing.

I hear moaning as I approach.

Now there is a good sign.

She looked like she had been run over by a caravan of trucks.

She is disoriented, weak, swollen, black and blue, and bloody, and am I so sorry that I am there.

Finally, her nurse (another perk) dresses her and sends her on her way with meds, prescriptions, samples of pain medicine, gauze icepacks (and that was only for me!).

Sam picks us up in front of the building, and then the gong rings.

It is five o'clock, time for rush hour and a very long ride home.

It is in the car, sitting in traffic, that I get the crushing blow.

Susannah announces that she can't go home.

"Sure you can," I say without faltering.

"Sam will not be able to give me the kind of care that I need," she continues.

"No one can give you the kind of care you need."

"That's right," chimes in Mr. iPhone champion.

He is only too happy to take care of his kids, or anybody's kids for that matter, rather than take care of his bride.

When Sam arrived at my house, he opened the door before we came to a full stop.

He sped away, lest Susannah change her mind.

I was exhausted and in some pain, but Susannah was the real mess.

We both walked tenuously up the stairs, and I looked at my watch.

Two hours and fifteen minutes and fifteen seconds on duty, before David could take over.

Susannah crawled into bed, and the orders ensued.

More pillows, bandage changes, painkillers for both of us, water.

Ma, you forgot the straw!

Down the stairs a million times.

On my fifteenth time up, I suggested that Susannah make a list so I could multitask. You should know that.

David saved Susannah's life that evening.

He came home seconds after Susannah announced that I wasn't doing a good job on her bandages.

Right before I was about to break her new nose.

"Here she is," I told David. "She's all yours."

I closed my bedroom door. On one hand I couldn't care if her nose fell off, but on the other hand, I wished I could take her pain.

We mothers belong to an unusual club, don't we?

I should add that this week I was on vacation from Pace, and by Wednesday, I longed to return. Susannah was able to breathe better through her nose, but she was unable to eat.

She lost six or seven pounds.

I called her nurse to find out if this was normal (now there's a good word for our family).

She reported that the average person loses between seven and nine pounds.

"Sign me up for Thursday," I told her.

After seeing this, you couldn't pay me enough to have a nose job or any other job.

The worst part of it all was that when most of the bandages were removed, she didn't love the result.

Now the nose looks great, but there are always people who try to make you feel much worse than you already feel.

Susannah left on Friday, and I relished being in my own space in my own house until I realized that it was time for Grandma (my mother-in-law) to stay for the weekend.

I am not even going there.

Susannah and I returned to our routine at about the same time.

She couldn't bend or lift (me too); both of us couldn't drive,

I must go back and comment on some of the reactions that I got when I returned to teaching after spring break.

One woman asked me if something was wrong with my neck (don't forget I was still in this brace).

No, I responded, I am practicing for a part.

Another idiot said to me, "I never saw you look so horrible."

Think back, I told her; there must have been a few times that you can remember, and don't forget to tell me.

Susannah received some nice commentary when she returned to the gym.

One of the best from these bitches was the woman who told her that she used to be so beautiful; what did she do to herself?

No filters today.

What's on their lung is on their tongue!

Love you so much,
Dr. Piggy

From: Mandel, Dr. Ellen
Sent: Sunday, April 25, 2013
To: Maxam, Dr. Susan L.
Subject: Insurance: friend or foe?

My dearest Dr. Wiggy,

After my accident on the twenty-first of March this year, the insurance company that represented the woman who plowed into me wanted to evaluate me.

I will refer to myself as the hittee (nonexistent term but I like it, and it is my story).

Moving on, my appointment was scheduled for May 28 at 2:00 p.m. at a nearby location.

How efficient could things be if I received four notices that were all the same within one week's time?

I approached cautiously, leaving only thirty minutes this time for getting lost.

Upon my arrival, I saw two men sitting in their respective cars and several people standing in the driveway.

A chiropractor's name was on a small shingle, but not so the insurance orthopedic surgeon (forgot to mention this wizard's title).

I got out of the car and stood around with the three others who were there before me.

Some person opened the office door to inform us that the doctor would be late.

What good news! And no, we could not come in and sit down.

A wise judgment, since it was a hot, sunny day and ninety-one degrees.

Another fifteen minutes passed, and many more people arrived, all of us sweltering.

Out of curiosity, I inquired, "How many of you have a two o'clock appointment?"

Twenty people raised their hands.

"Don't worry," I said a few minutes after.

Sixteen of us or more will die of sunstroke and will no longer be able to articulate our injuries to this clever doctor.

At 2:20 p.m. this doctor arrived, and lo and behold, there were not enough seats in his office for all of us.

Musical chairs on an afternoon that was becoming more entertaining as the afternoon wore on.

We signed in and were given clipboards with five sheets of paper to complete.

I always find the "Could you be pregnant?" question so pertinent for me.

The selection of the order was based on how quickly you could complete the forms and turn them in at the front desk.

Since seats were at a premium, it was not surprising when people did not want to get up and chance losing their seat.

I still was not expecting this three-hundred-plus-pound woman to point her finger at me and say with an angry face, "Listen, girl, don't mess with me. You watch this seat until I come back from the toilet. You hear me?"

Everyone heard her.

And being the devout coward that I am, I responded quickly.

"Lady, I will watch whatever you want for as long as you want, because you have a scary face!"

The room was filled with laughter, but I knew in my heart that this woman meant business.

I forgot to mention that the two men who were outside in their cool cars who waited to come in were punished for not waiting on the scalding black tar, and they were seen after the first twenty others.

At last my name was called.

The examination was thorough and efficient!

The doctor hit both of my patellas, asked me to bend my neck forward and then backward, told me I was wearing a great color nail polish, and made no attempt to hear any of my complaints.

With this I am sure that he found no need to continue any of my treatments.

I was worried about a doctor who no doubt got his degree at Sears or from a nineteenth world country.

The names have remained a secret to protect the guilty.

One other comment here.

I am sure that I will be long dead before I will collect my three dollars from my accident!

Love you,
Dr. Piggy

From: Mandel, Dr. Ellen
Sent: Monday, February 19, 2014, 5:46 p.m.
To: Maxam, Dr. Susan L.
Subject: Dr. Coo-Coo Bird

My dearest Dr. VP and everything else Wiggy,

Today a very sick Dr. Piggy decided it was time to confirm her diagnosis of a bad case of bronchitis.

After a couple of days, I thought it might be a good idea to actually see a physician.

The fact that this bronchitis is superimposed upon my other condition, acid reflux with esophageal spasms, made a bad situation worse.

And since I can make just about any situation worse, this was my day to shine!

Previous to a few years ago, one had a slight chance of seeing your designated doctor in the group, with only a little whining and a few threats to the receptionist.

Today with all the new hoopla, the receptionist told me that I could see my own doctor on March 5.

But I am very sick on February 19, I responded.

How about seeing our newest doctor?

This office has had a slew of doctors, besides the original group, whose names don't even make it to the list on the door.

I told them to list the names in pencil. I agreed to see the newest one, whom I shall call Dr. Coo-Coo Bird. He claimed I had hypertension. Funny, I said, I consistently run 90/60.

But you are taking a high blood pressure pill. But I am using it as a mild diuretic. It was given to me by my cardiologist.

Maybe you have a urinary infection, he suggested. Maybe I have tonsillitis, even though I don't have tonsils, I thought to myself.

Dr. Coo-Coo Bird wanted to chat, and I couldn't get out of the office fast enough.

I wouldn't even list him in pencil!

Similarly, my Susannah, about three weeks ago, had a terrible sore throat. She was a little achy but no fever.

She couldn't see our regular doctor either. (You can only see him for well checkups, I found out.)

She was given this foreign doctor who was barely intelligible. He diagnosed her as having the flu and didn't prescribe an antibiotic. I want one, Susannah told him, because I think I have strep.

The doctor didn't take this well, and he turned red in the face and started to stamp his feet (an unusual hissy fit if I ever saw one).

He reluctantly cultured her upon her insistence.

You know what happened of course. She had strep. Thank God she was smart enough to start her mother's emergency supply of amoxicillin!

Before I close, let me tell you that today was Matthew's eighth birthday, and I was too sick to go to the party and eat all the kids' leftover cupcake parts.

But I sang him the Happy Birthday song, and was so thrilled that he listened to the whole song. I asked him if he knew how much his Nanny loved him, and he said he knew.

What a big boy and what a mensch he is.

Another instance of grandchildren making you heart sing.

A true gift from God that I wish on everyone. The joy of joys!

Love u,
Dr. Piggy

From: Mandel, Dr. Ellen
Sent: Wednesday, March 19, 2014, 4:23 p.m.
To: Maxam, Dr. Susan L.
Subject: Dr. Protectors

Dear Dr. Wiggy,

Today is the cortisone shot for my shoulder. I arrived promptly.

The nurse told me that people faint from time to time.

There's a good way to begin!

The shot was yucky but I stayed on my feet, too embarrassed to do much else.

I was given new meds to add to my medication arsenal and dismissed.

Only if this persists must I return in two weeks for an MRI. Now, a few words about many of today's doctors are appropriate here!

It is unfortunate that there are a multitude of doctors and nurses who do not fall into the fabulous category. These doctors have begun to see thousands more patients and all at the same appointment time. Patients used to be booked on the half hour. Now it's the seven- or eight-minute special.

If I have four symptoms, they only have time for you to tell about two.

The last two can be discussed at the next appointment. You will be seen at 9:20 a.m., and you are down for two symptoms, reports the receptionist.

"The doctor is not happy today," she adds. Tell him his patient is not too happy either, since I am sick as a dog.

Can you imagine? I call this breed of nurses "doctor protectors."

They shield the doctors from you.

I once had a doctor protector who was very avant-garde.

I asked to speak to the doctor when I called (in those days sometimes doctors actually walked three steps to the phone and spoke with you).

She replied that the doctor was running late and couldn't possibly speak to me, and then the best line of all:

"You probably have a virus."

"Really?" I said. "And where did you get your medical degree?" I screeched.

"That's ridiculous," she yelled into the phone.

"Not any more ridiculous than your giving me my diagnosis," I yelled back and hung up before I suffered from a hot case of apoplexy.

Love you, Dr. Wiggy.
Smell the roses!
Dr. Piggy

From: Mandel, Dr. Ellen
Sent: Sunday, June 1, 2014, 3:20 p.m.
To: Maxam, Dr. Susan L.
Subject: God drives home.

Friday morning was similar to many a morning, with the exception being that Susannah and I got to start our shopping adventure a little earlier than usual. Susannah is a clothes horse, and me just the horse part.

Jews all over the world are forbidden in the Bible to buy anything at full price. Even if you buy something, you really don't quite need, at least you got it at a fabulous price.

Susannah and I love, love, love Foxes. They get new merchandise every day.

I live vicariously. My beautiful daughter looks beautiful in everything (size two or four), and there are usually three or four garments in my size (not a ten; that's the highest I can articulate).

Of the three or four, there are usually two I hate, two I like, and maybe one that fits or almost fits.

I am forced to buy a lot of earrings.

The salespeople know us quite well and are overjoyed to see us, especially Susannah, who makes me look like a nonshopper.

I did better twenty-five years and twenty-five pounds ago in the now-defunct-and-yet-famous Loehman's.

I was such a good Loehman's shopper that when my mother died, the company sent me a huge basket of fruit!

Well on this Friday, I found three garments.

I was ecstatic.

We were all ready to pay when the bad phone call came.

My husband, David, was on the phone.

He had gone to the cardiologist that morning because he had the same sensation that he had gotten when he needed stents. This sensation sometimes signaled trouble and other times not.

I am never permitted to accompany him, because I tend not to be able to behave.

The doctor asks, "How is you eating?"

David replies great, and a small or not-so-small voice replies, "He eats terribly." It's been a couple of years now since I've been banished.

In any case, no good news!

David's electrocardiogram and echocardiogram were bizarre.

That's a word our family hears rather often.

Our great Dr. Kennish sent him right over to our condo, Mt. Sinai, for an emergency cardiogram.

I skip unsettled and go right to hysterical.

Susannah and I leave the store immediately. She and I drive in her massive truck right into the city.

One of my saddest moments of the day—no time to pay for my two garments that fit.

We arrived at 1468 Madison Avenue, fifth floor, room 182, only to find that David has been sent to the prep room.

We will be able to see him in ninety minutes, before he goes up for the procedure.

It is now many hours later. We have seen him before he goes in.

Kisses and a few tears from all parties.

Less than an hour later, patient taken to recovery.

No stent!

Hurrah, hurrah!

What were the cardiac anomalies? No one knows.

That's reassuring!

We will find out on Monday.

After a stent, or nonstent, I know from too much experience that the patient must remain perfectly still.

It also means no driving for three days.

It finally hits me.

OMG, Susannah is a great driver, but she has only one tuchus and can only drive her car home, not David's.

That leaves me.

Reasons for me to panic:

1) Terrible driver
2) Never have driven David's new car, because I make new cars old instantly
3) Night blindness
4) Cataract in right eye creates rainbows in front of my eyes at night
5) Driving always a hundred times worse when David directs me

Outcome

I informed the nurse that David would be leaving at 8:00 p.m. whether he was ready or not.

He would hold his groin for the whole trip.

After not needing the stent, I continued, why should he get killed in the car?

She couldn't agree with us more.

I brought the car around in front of the door, he was there at two minutes to eight, and off we went.

Only the last twelve minutes of our ride was I totally blind, and God drove the rest of the way, with me pretending to see.

All my love,
Dr. Piggy (motor enthusiast)

CHAPTER 9

Cancer: An Unwelcome Visitor

From: Mandel, Dr. Ellen
Sent: Friday, August 8, 2014, 5:49 a.m.
To: Maxam, Dr. Susan L.
Subject: Leukemia—an unwelcome visitor

My dearest Dr. Wiggy,

Mama, without her college degree, was one smart cookie!

She always said that one's life could change in one split second. On July 22 I went to Quest blood labs to have a full blood panel of tests taken to see if I was right in my diagnosis of hyperthyroid.

Having had Hashimoto's thyroid disease for nearly forty years, I find that every so often my Synthroid medication needs a little tweaking.

The results were sent to my wonderful internist/cardiologist.

I walked into his office the following day, July 23, smugly, knowing almost for sure that my diagnosis was correct.

And so it was hyperthyroidism.

I came to this conclusion since the night sweats, which I have been having for years, were turning into day sweats as well.

After nearly breaking my arm patting myself on the back, I left the office.

There were still a few tests pending, and the doctor said that he would call me as soon as those results came in if there were a problem.

I was so anxious to get out of the city and beat the traffic.

It follows you wherever you go!

Arriving in Rockland, I wasted no time in getting the new prescription filled and arrived home just in time to pick up the kitchen phone that was ringing.

"The doctor would like to speak to you," the voice said.

Not thinking that he called to discuss the weather, I became instantly concerned.

"Ellen," the voice said. "I have terrible news. I have to tell you," he continued, "because I need you to turn around right now and come back into the city and see the doctor who will be waiting for you."

When is there ever a doctor waiting for you to arrive?

Answer to that question: never.

"You have leukemia," he continued.

I took down the information and headed over to my kitchen chair, because I knew I was going to pass out.

Got up slowly, got a glass of water, and went into emergency mode.

My husband never leaves his cell phone on. (I've threatened to kill him many times.)

So I left three urgent messages at his office, adding don't worry, it's not your mother.

Called my daughter, who began four days of nonstop crying, and my sister, Sooz.

Left the dishwasher open, coffee in the microwave, and ran out of the house.

My daughter drove me to the oncologist, going about eighty miles an hour.

Now, that was a brilliant idea.

She needn't have rushed to see the doctor who was waiting for us, because this doctor kept us waiting for two and a half hours.

My husband met us at the office, and we waited.

The office was not inviting.

It looked like a large factory.

So sorry that I had to go to the ladies' room, because I saw a small room stuffed with people hooked up to chemo.

What terrible club was I becoming a member of?

Finally we were seen by this lovely oncologist, who looked as if she just graduated grade school.

That's pretty much how it appears, now that I am in my late sixties.

She took seven vials of blood, and as nuts as I was, I didn't spare her my Pop-Pop's corniest joke.

"Gee, I thought I was a blue blood."

Remembering my Pop-Pop was somehow comforting.

I didn't shed a tear. I, who am always chopped liver and cry at the blink of an eye for everyone, was all of a sudden brave.

Who was this person whose life would never be the same?

Love you,
Dr. Piggy

From: Mandel, Dr. Ellen
Sent: Saturday, August 9, 2014, 5:46 p.m.
To: Maxam, Dr. Susan L.
Subject: Choosing an oncologist

Choosing an oncologist was the next step, and it was a little like choosing a dress for Susannah's wedding. I had to see the best selection, and the dress had to be the best fit and the most comfortable. The first oncologist, who by the way initially confirmed my diagnosis of leukemia and gave me the bone-marrow test the following day, was lovely, but not for me. We did have to pick up the reports in order to have them for Doctor Number Two. We parked in a garage uptown and walked the rest of the way.

With the reports in hand, we returned to the garage that had the colossal nerve to charge us sixty-three dollars. (We are all in the wrong business.)

As we arrived to claim our car, Princess Susannah announced that she was going to faint if she didn't get something to eat immediately from the Fairway Supermarket right next to the garage.

Was there any doubt what we did next?

I think not.

We flew into Fairway, and she bought some sushi. Then we walked back to the garage next door.

The garage was steamy. It was around eighty-seven degrees and humid.

Susannah sat on the dirty garage waiting area floor and began to eat. She could have had a ten-course meal, actually, because there were ten cars ahead of us (absolutely no use of hyperbole).

To make matters worse, in that cavernous bag of hers, she could not locate the parking ticket.

I didn't even have time to gasp, when this toothless, disheveled, homeless man approached me and asked me to buy him lunch.

While I heard Susannah negotiating the price of the car, without the ticket found, I whipped out a five-dollar bill for the poor man's lunch.

"No, lady," he announced. "I want you to take me food shopping at Fairway." That's what I needed now, a shopping spree at Fairway with a homeless person.

"Sorry, bud," I said. "There is no way in hell I am taking you food shopping now."

I held out my hand once again, with the five spot.

He was very unhappy, but not too unhappy to take my money and run.

By this time, Lady Godiva was feeling better, having eaten sushi all over the dirty floor, and my car finally arrived.

I was dripping wet when we began our trek home.

I will describe these other visits, but I need to provide some clarification.

How this went down at the time was dramatic and humorous, just like my life is.

But this was serious business, and I am no fool.

I was and am frightened of the road ahead.

Am I brave? I rather think I am.

But I can't promise anything to myself or anybody else, until we are farther down the line.

If I am dealing with lots of discomfort and/or pain or unexpected detours in this already bumpy road, I will not be a happy camper.

I want the impossible.

I want it to be July 22, before my life changed forever.

Have to mention, once again, how my family has been unbelievably wonderful.

Thank you, God! And thank you, my delicious family.

This doesn't mean that Leigh could move back home! I'm not that grateful!

The next day, it was David's turn to schlep the old lady into the city for the second consult, at one of the most famous cancer treatment hospitals in the world. We met with one of the most famous leukemia specialists in the world as well.

Upon entering the waiting room, we saw everyone wearing these surgical masks.

A confrontation with reality and a humbling experience.

As we waited our turn, one woman thought it might be helpful to tell me, in great detail, about her three bone-marrow transplants. Some people are just morons and should keep their mouths shut. (Maybe she works as a telephone operator; last week this halfwit woman asked me if New York City is in New York. I replied no; they just moved it to New Jersey).

They called my name, and I went into this little room to give more blood.

Then the consult. The doctor was a brilliant, well-informed person and very nice to me.

When I left, I told David and Sooz (I forgot to mention that Sooz met us there) that I couldn't pinpoint it, but this wasn't the perfect fit.

One more consult to go, and the list was shrinking.

Would I even know if I found what I was looking for?

Two days later we arrived at New York Presbyterian Hospital at 165th Street and Fort Washington Place.

A million more forms to fill out, more blood to give.

No wonder why leukemia patients often become anemic. How much blood could one tired lady have?

We waited our turn once again, and I had to use the ladies' room.

I hadn't made a fool of myself yet that day, so I proceeded to lock myself in the bathroom. I banged on the door, and a lovely nurse came to my aid and instructed me on how to extricate myself from the damn toilet.

I did feel better, I must admit, when she told me that somebody does that every day (well, not that much better).

My David, of course, was not the least bit surprised (well, so what!).

I was finally ushered into the office of Dr. Gregory Mears, a tall, burly Irishman with a twinkle in his eye.

Very professional, but with a kind face and manner. He was so positive that he could help me.

Five minutes into our meeting, I knew I had found the right "wedding dress"—the perfect fit and comfortable.

And of course I felt compelled to announce it.

"You're my new doctor," I said, "if you'll take me."

And the search was over.

He's probably wondering what he did to deserve me, don't you think?

Of course he was leaving for vacation for two weeks, but he laid out the regime, and I would start the oral meds in his absence.

I discussed my concern with the assorted sides that might be coming my way within the next few weeks.

As a rehabilitated bulimic, I told him that I would sign up for the bleeding eye as opposed to the weight gain.

"Why do I believe you, Dr. Mandel?" he asked.

"Because I mean it," I replied.

Xxxooo,
Dr. Piggy

From: Mandel, Dr. Ellen
Sent: Sunday, August 10, 2014, 9:14 p.m.
To: Maxam, Dr. Susan L.
Subject: A miracle drug with a miracle price

The drug that I began taking seven days ago cost $25,000 a month, or $860 per pill.

I will never complain about my insurance company again—well, maybe hardly ever. Thank God I am covered. What happens to those people who aren't covered?

Do they just die? Terrifying possibility.

The sides come after a few weeks. I am so frightened of the unknown.

I do know that whether it be from the leukemia or the treatment, I am very tired and can't run around all day the way I used to.

It drives me crazy, but you realize quite quickly that you can tantrum all you want, but you must make accommodations. You have no choice. I try to do all my very important things in the morning and afternoon and save the rest for the next day,

Do I want to live this way? No!

But I do want to live!

All my love,
Dr. Piggy, the scared warrior

From: Mandel, Dr. Ellen
Sent: Thursday, August 14, 2014, 7:11 a.m.
To: Maxam, Dr. Susan L.
Subject: Don't ever bite the bullet.

Good morning, my vacationing Dr. Wiggy,

Hope you're having a fabulous vacation.

Nobody deserves it more!

Ten or so days into the oral meds, and not much in the way of side effects yet.

I am happy until I can't be happy and enjoying each day to the max!

I love these people who tell you the flowers look brighter, the sky bluer—what a crock!

I always appreciated what as a child I called a "blue and yellow" crystal-blue sky and radiant sunshine!

I was asked if I am noticing more things around me. Actually, yes.

Yesterday, I noticed that one of my neighbors on Strawtown Road has a stuffed bulldog dressed in a Santa outfit with Christmas lights attached to him.

An ugly Santa boxer in August.

Now there is a fellow who has it all together!

On to other things, I should really entitle this snippet "How I nearly got killed from the bullet."

Let me explain why…

As soon as I received that enviable diagnosis of CML (chronic myeloid leukemia), I thought about seeing someone to help me develop a healthier eating style (although I must admit, that the cake diet has always served me well).

When I was stupid enough to consult the net and came face-to-face with this unhappy woman's commentary about gaining thirty pounds from Sprycel, my drug, in nine months, I contacted a nutritional oncologist whom I knew from twenty-five years ago.

She was practicing oncology with a holistic slant.

I met with her lovely colleagues, who helped me flesh out the perfect regime for me.

"Sugar has got to go except in the smallest quantity," she announced. I was able to negotiate six M&Ms a day. High protein, high fat, almost no carbs, and lots and lots of veggies.

As if it weren't bad enough having cancer!

Two tablespoons of omega oil daily and lots of olive oil.

She suggested that I purchase the Nutribullet, this juicing wonder, to liquefy the veggies.

Good student that I am, I began on my foreign healthy journey.

With the Bed Bath and Beyond five-dollar coupon, I purchased that Nutribullet for seventy-six dollars.

The special omega oil, thirty-two dollars; the vitamin, thirty-five dollars.

Now to the supermarket! Spinach, kale, chard (what the hell is chard?), broccoli, green apples, done.

The next morning I juiced using this Nutribullet. The resulting masterpiece looked like a puree, not a juice. I drank it anyway. It was disgusting. Then on to the tablespoon of omega oil.

That was far worse than the horrific veggies.

I kept this up for two days.

Bloated, constipated, a little nauseous, and a little more acid. (I have acid reflux, among all my lovely conditions.)

On day three, my husband and I went up to Cold Springs, New York, for a much-needed day of R and R.

After about an hour, I began to feel really sick. I had cramps, followed by diarrhea and vomiting. I turned a nice shade of green.

On my return home—we all know the saying—first I was afraid I was going to die, and then I was afraid I was going to live.

Love,
Dr. Piggy

About the Author

Ellen Mandel grew up in the Flatbush section of Brooklyn. Upon her graduation, her parents gave her the choice of attending any college in the country—as long as it was Brooklyn College. There she received a BA and MS in speech pathology.

After ten years practicing speech therapy and teaching at Pace University, Mandel received her doctorate from Columbia University, picking up an MPhil along the way. During her time at Pace, she won many awards for teaching excellence, including the Carol Russet Award for Women in Higher Education. She retired in 2015.

Ellen works closely with the Susan G. Komen Foundation, among other organizations, and has received the prestigious Jefferson Award for her lifelong service.

Married to her childhood sweetheart, Dr. David Mandel, for forty-eight years, Ellen is the mother of two wonderful children, Leigh and Susannah, and has two beautiful grandchildren, Matthew and Jacob.

42380055R00096

Made in the USA
Middletown, DE
11 April 2017